E PLURIBUS UNUM
Out of Many. . . One

A Pictorial Presentation
Of A Journey
From Fragmentation To Integration

Sandy Sela-Smith, Ph.D.
Benjamin B. Keyes, Ph.D.

Manitou Communications, Inc.

www.manitoucommunications.com
www.rossinst.com
rossinst@rossinst.com

Designed by Deep River Design
www.deepriverdesign.com

ISBN: 0-9704525-7-8

Printed in China

Library of Congress Card Number: 2003111231

Sela-Smith, Sandy
Keyes, Benjamin

E Pluribus Unum: Out Of Many. . . One

ISBN: 0-9704525-7-8

1. Psychotherapy   2. Dissociative Identity Disorder   3. Recovery

DEDICATION

To a nine-month-old baby who was identified in local newspapers only with the nickname Mooka*, whose real name I may never know. This infant was kidnapped, beaten, and raped very early in the morning of September 21, 2001. Her little body was covered over with twigs and leaves and her assailant left her for dead in a wooded area in Tampa, Florida. In spite of all the odds against it, this little child clung to life, and she survived. Searchers heard her cry and saw her tiny hand reaching out from the brush that was intended to be her grave. Her courage to free herself from the hands of death, gave me the courage to not give up on life when the events of 9-11-2001 touched my own childhood struggles and caused me to nearly lose hope for humanity. To Mooka and all the Mookas of this world, I dedicate this book.

Dr. Sandy Sela-Smith

I want to dedicate this book to all the brave clients who struggle to overcome what seem to be insurmountable obstacles in their healing. I want to thank those who have chosen to allow me the privilege of traveling some of the distance with them. Healing is very possible and can be very real.

Dr. Benjamin B. Keyes

*The nickname is part of the public domain, as printed in the story of the child in the *Tampa Tribune*, September 23, 2001.

TABLE OF CONTENTS

THE STORY BEHIND THE MAPPING

The Mind Maps

MULTIPLE LEVELS / MULTIPLE SELVES

COLLAPSE OF THE LEVELS

COLLAPSE OF THE SEPARATIONS

OUT OF MANY. . . ONE

Sandy Sela-Smith, Ph.D., Benjamin B. Keyes, Ph.D.

ACKNOWLEDGEMENTS

BK: I want to thank Sandy Sela-Smith for the honor of traveling with her as a client, and now as a colleague and friend. A special thanks goes to Colin Ross who believed in this project enough to help get it published, and whose insight, lectures, teachings, and friendship have helped to train and guide me over the years. Thank you to Becky Eddy and Lara Knox and to important friends and mentors who have influenced my thinking, challenged my stubbornness and supported me through the years. They include: Carol Parker, Murray Landsman, Roy Persons, Pincus Gross, Bill Layton, Kathie Erwin, Ron Droz, Jan Ladd, Michael VanButsel, Sterling Dimmtt, Natalie Keyes, Scott and Cyndi Bruner, Sandy Brown, Dale Dunham, Margaret Heller, Carol Lynn Yancar, Bennett Braun, Richard Kluft, Karen Moorhead, Hank DeWeerd, Linda Stevenson, Rick Pettey, Ram Das, Dwight Gilbert, Seth and Sally Keyes, Gertrude Krause, Mort Whitman, T.J. Thompson, Jim Noble, David Swindall, Joyce Hutchens, Andrea Dourm, and Joan Hurlbut.

Finally, a thank you to Shawn and Jasmin who have inspired me to grow beyond myself.

SS: I want to thank Ben Keyes for asking me a decade ago to draw a picture of what I was seeing. If he had not done that, though I have no doubt that I still would have healed, the healing might not have occurred as quickly as it did, and likely, not as consciously. And most importantly in this context, *E Pluribus Unum* would not have been written as it is presented here. Of course, I want to express my appreciation to Colin Ross for being patient in all the back and forth work to get this book published, and many thanks to Keleigh Milliorn for her remarkable design work that so beautifully presents *E Pluribus Unum*. I also want to thank those people who were able to see my strength when I felt only weakness, who were able to see my wholeness when all I experienced of myself was one who was broken, and who were willing to let me laugh as well as cry in the process of becoming one. These include: Anne Martin, Ben Turner, Bill Stampler, Carol Bates, David Baty, David Illig, David Klein, David Tai, Don Boehm, Don Parks, Esther Klein, Kathryn Day, Linda Montgomery, Lorna Minewiser, Lydia Hammond, Michael Maskornick, Sarah Goodwin, Stanley Krippner, Steven Feldman, Terry Waters, Tim Brady, and three of my dear four legged friends: Jenny, Rachael, and Sara.

FOREWORD

E Pluribus Unum is a unique contribution to the field. No other book describes the therapy of dissociative identity disorder through a combination of words and pictures. Also, no other book takes the reader inside the therapy from two perspectives, that of the therapist and that of the client. There is a third feature of *E Pluribus Unum* that makes it a triply unique document: the client, Dr. Sela-Smith, has been integrated for ten years. Following her integration in 1994, Dr. Sela-Smith earned a Ph.D. in psychology, obtained a Professorship, set up and ran a private practice, and spoke and published professionally. All of these activities are ongoing. This is a story of recovery and triumph.

As everyone in the field knows too well, the diagnosis and treatment of dissociative identity disorder have been under attack in the media, the courts and the professional literature for over a decade. Virtually all elements of the therapy have been mocked and devalued, including mapping, talking directly with alter personalities, guided imagery, journaling, art therapy and memory recovery. This book provides a counter to those attacks. The devalued aspects of treatment lead to full recovery in this case. The recovery is undeniable, objective and functional.

E Pluribus Unum teaches several other important lessons as well. No matter what the extreme critics and armchair quarterbacks have to say about therapy, it is not always tidy and orderly, and the therapist does not have control of the process. The therapist can guide, shape and consult, but cannot control. In real therapy, in the real world, the process guides the interventions as much as the interventions guide the process. Flashbacks occur, body memories occur, God is involved, and there are many complex interactions in the internal landscape. This is how it is in real therapy.

Dr. Sela-Smith's psychotherapy illustrates a crucial point about the false memory wars. The therapy provided by Dr. Keyes could be attacked as typical "recovered memory therapy" but it was profoundly helpful. It led to stabilization, integration and healing. You couldn't ask for a better outcome.

This book will help the field be less defensive. Many of our techniques and principles have been attacked by critics who claim to be "scientific" but who are in fact simply hostile ideologists. Here we have a detailed record of a successful treatment that counters the idea that "recovered memory therapy" is always bad. Of course, "recovered memory therapy" is a straw man invented by the extreme critics. Dr. Keyes does not practice this non-existent method of therapy, although many memories were recovered during the process. Whether these memories are mostly accurate or contain significant distortions is irrelevant from a treatment outcome perspective. Outcome was superb. Given that fact, the question of the accuracy of the memories is not important.

As a field, I think, we have been drawn into a false debate that is based on a false premise. It has not been a real debate; rather, it has been a series of intellectualized drive-by shootings. There have been casualties in the false memory wars. As long as the memory content is contained within the therapy, its accuracy is a minor consideration in the overall planning, conduct and outcome of psychotherapy. *E Pluribus Unum* proves this point at the single case level. It is a lesson the field needs to internalize – needs to integrate. Dr. Sela-Smith's therapeutic work with Dr. Keyes could be pilloried as stereotypical "recovered memory therapy." The engineers of the pillory must account for one anomalous observation, however – her full recovery.

Colin A. Ross, M.D.
March 22, 2004

HOW THIS BOOK CAME TO BE

As fall of 2002 neared, Dr. Sandy Sela-Smith and Dr. Benjamin Keyes dusted off a manuscript that had been untouched for nearly seven years. The original text was written in late 1994, in the form of a script entitled *From Fragmentation to Integration* that Dr. Keyes used to introduce a series of slides of drawings that had been done by Sandy, over the course of her integration therapy from early 1993 to mid 1994. Sandy was his client at the time. These drawings portrayed the process of her healing from what was then called Multiple Personality Disorder (MPD), now identified as Dissociative Identity Disorder (DID). Ben had presented his material at conferences in the United States and in Australia. Later, Sandy had prepared her own script and presented her healing process at a conference in Manchester, England for the UK branch of the International Society for the Study of Dissociation in 1999. The book, as it appears now, represents an integration of the two presentations.

Sandy's focus in writing was on her experience of healing, while Ben's focus was on the therapeutic method of mind mapping as a way to direct the healing process. Sandy called her contribution *E Pluribus Unum*, which in Latin means *out of many, one*. These words symbolizing her experience are the words engraved on American coins, referring to the fact that the United States of America is one nation formed out of many states.

Ben called his contribution to the writing *Fragmentation to Integration,* identifying the features and uses of the mind map as a therapeutic tool with dissociative clients. Together the two perspectives narrate a story of wounding and healing that is intended to help therapists in their work with clients whose histories lead to dissociation, and to help clients who suffered early-life trauma that led to the experience of fragmentation of the self.

The manuscript was essentially completed in 1995, but at the time, seeking publication was not a priority. Sandy was involved in graduate studies that would lead to a Master's degree in 1999 and a Ph.D. in psychology in 2001. After her graduation as a doctor of psychology and certification as a mental health counselor in Florida, Sandy became a published author and a professor at Saybrook Graduate School in San Francisco. She also began a research project with the Geffen Cancer Center in Vero Beach, Florida, using Heuristic Self-Search Inquiry, a research method she formulated while in graduate school, to investigate the impact of psycho-spiritual healing on the life-experience of cancer patients. Ben had become involved in a joint research project with Colin A. Ross regarding dissociation among patients in the People's Republic of China. Results of this project were presented in China in the summer of 2002.

By the winter of 2002-03, both Ben and Sandy, whose relationship shifted in the intervening years from therapist/client to professional colleagues and friends, finally were free to give attention to the story that had been told so simply, yet powerfully in a series of drawings, so many years before. In the past fifteen or twenty years, numerous stories have been recorded of the horrors of childhood abuse and the destructive impact that such abuse has had on the lives of its victims. However, there are very few stories that focus on the path that leads through the devastation to the other side where full healing occurs, and where the person and the life of the one who had been the victim of abuse, have become victoriously transformed. *E Pluribus Unum, From Fragmentation to Integration* is such a story.

THE STORY
BEHIND THE MAPPING

THE STORY
BEHIND THE MAPPING

The Client's Perspective
Sandy Sela-Smith, Ph.D.

On a comfortable and sunny February morning in 1993 I placed a call to Dr. Benjamin Keyes, a psychotherapist in Clearwater, Florida, known for his skillful work with Multiple Personality Disorder (MPD), now identified by the American Psychiatric Association as Dissociative Identity Disorder (DID). I was inquiring to see if Dr. Keyes would be available to work with me to complete the unfinished therapy that I had begun in 1986. My therapeutic work had gone unattended from 1990 to 1993 during which time I had lived in China for nearly two years and afterward relocated from the Northwest to the Southeast of the United States. I was pleased to find out that Dr. Keyes would be willing to begin seeing me as a client. At the time of that February phone call, my first name was San Dy. My name had been split in two at birth and recorded as two names on my birth certificate in 1944, perhaps an unconscious metaphor created by my parents that revealed the life path upon which my infant-self was about to embark.

Beginnings in the Middle of My Life

Stress related to difficult life events in 1985 began to crack the outer shell that had kept my world intact for nearly four decades. In that devastating year, I began experiencing unbearable headaches, reminiscent of the headaches that brought me to specialists when I was fifteen. These sharp and piercing headaches, both in my teen years and in my adult life were physically debilitating. Later in my life, I became aware that when I was younger the headaches were followed by periods when I lost my awareness of time; when young, I had no idea that this was happening. After the headaches began dominating my life, I started doing things that were unlike the person I had always known myself to be. Following a frightening panic attack and physical collapse that I experienced in the office that I shared with my husband in our business sometime in early 1986, I left the business that we jointly owned and never returned.

The collapse led me to seek psychological help in 1986, and sometime in the first months of therapy, I was diagnosed as having Multiple Personality Disorder. Over the next four years my life felt as if it had turned upside down, and inside out, and had shattered into a thousand pieces. The first three years of therapy were with David, a clinical psychologist in the Northwest. He supported me as I struggled with events that eventually led to the disintegration of my outer world and a growing awareness of the shattered multiplicity of my inner world. A few months after the diagnosis, I filed for divorce and got an apartment where I lived in almost total solitude for three years. There were times I spent weeks in my apartment, leaving only for therapy appointments and walking my dog. It was not unusual for a trip to the store for groceries to end abruptly with a half-filled basket left along an aisle. For some unexplainable reason I would be unable to complete the shopping or go through the checkout line. All I could do was rush home as quickly as possible, empty handed. On occasion, the only thing that forced me to stay in a line was if I had run out of dog food.

It was not unusual for me to spend an entire day in isolation, sitting in a Papasan chair staring out into nothingness. The spell could have been broken by a telephone ring, or the paw of my puppy who was reminding me that she was hungry. I had taught her to relieve herself on something called Pee-Pee Pads as a way to protect me from having to go outside during the day when I might have to see people. I ignored the ringing of the telephone, but the hunger cry of my puppy would break through, letting me know that night had come, bringing with it the safety of dark shadows that filled the silence of my room.

Even the stereo and television were unwanted invasions of my self-imposed isolation. Newspapers, not even removed from their plastic delivery containers, piled up next to the front door for weeks at a time. It seemed as if any movement, any connection to the outer world, even a call to cancel the paper, created a sense of overload.

Memories long forgotten had begun leaking through, disrupting the order I had so carefully created to cover the inner chaos. It was difficult enough to deal with the collapse of my marriage, the demise of my professional life, and the disintegration of the foundations of my life without having to handle what seemed to be incomprehensible horrors of childhood. Much of the time was spent denying the leakage and doing all I could to stop it from coming forward.

Finally, after three years of intense struggle, I permitted entrance into an inner space that seemed to be a dark and seemingly abandoned compound filled with damaged parts of myself. Children who had been hiding in blackened rooms for decades were terrified of the dark, yet afraid to be seen in the light. With David's guidance, I walked the corridors and brought in a message that I had come to help them become free. This connection was a major breakthrough in my therapy. At the end of that third year, just as the first concrete connection with the inside system had been made, personal concerns of my therapist resulted in his decision to move out of state. This person whom I had finally learned to trust with the overwhelming condition of my inner world was leaving. I was devastated.

Somewhere in the middle of my work with David, I began body therapy with Michael. He had an innate sense of my inner world, and was able to help me transition through the completion of the first phase of therapy that ended with David's departure and into the inauguration of the second phase beginning with another psychotherapist a few months later. This second phase of therapy began when I found Steven, who sat with me two sessions each week during which time I dropped into horrific childhood experiences that I was no longer able hold back. The long repressed memories of physical, emotional, and sexual abuse flowed out of me in what seemed like unending streams of horror.

Day and night, week after week, memories of a lifetime of violence and abuse erupted in what were often intolerably overwhelming abreactions. Everything in the outer world that I saw, touched, smelled, heard, or experienced became the conduit for exposing long repressed memories. My nights were filled with unbearable dreams and night-shocks; my days were spent reacting to life itself as memories flooded in, leaving my nerves ravaged, my mind strained to exhaustion, and my body feeling as if it had been torn open, exposing pulsing unstoppable pain.

I would have preferred to believe that I had gone insane than to accept the horrors that began to emerge. There were many times I left the therapy office still in an in-between place not fully submerged in the middle of an unbearable memory but not yet back in the present. Sometimes I sat in my car for an hour or two waiting for the memory to fade and for the strength to press the gas pedal. Other times I found myself home without remembering how I got there.

As the memories came back, I made connection with a sister with whom I had been out of contact for almost a decade. She had been in therapy for a number of years living in her own isolation with memories that we were soon to discover matched those that were now coming up for me. With the confirmations in her story and her drawings that were parallel to my own memories, I could no longer reject what I was learning about my childhood years, a childhood that we shared together. For the first time in eight years, she was getting confirmation of events that she, too, had preferred to be the conjuring of her insane mind. Our separate and previously unshared memories and flashbacks were too similar to discount.

Body Messages

My body had been revealing the childhood secrets throughout my life, but I had not been attuned to its messages. I had developed endometriosis when I was still a teenager with menstrual periods that left me nearly incapacitated. In my early adult years I had five miscarriages. I had the beginnings of uterine cancer that required D & C procedures and a freezing procedure called cryosurgery. Vaginal and uterine infections were ongoing. Kidney and bladder infections were constantly a part of my life causing urination to be a painful, burning experience from at least the time I was five. All of this finally resulted in hospitalization for a system-wide infection in early 1980 that nearly cost me my life. These can all be indicators of sexual abuse - but I did not know that at the time.

All of these difficulties were followed by a medical recommendation for a hysterectomy in my mid-thirties. A second hospitalization in that same year resulted in an operation to remove extensive scarring and urethra blockage, common in women with a sexual abuse history. Rectal scarring made bowel movements an almost unbearable experience as far back as I could remember. I had always assumed that bodily elimination was supposed to be painful.

From my early teens, I suffered from intense migraine headaches often lasting for days at a time. During those bouts, a tingling numbness began in my fingertips and proceeded up my arms across my shoulders, up my neck, and to my face. When the numbness reached the center of my face, nausea and often dry gagging began, followed by the unrelenting headache, and often periods of blindness. The only respite could be found by going into a darkened room, covering my head with a pillow, becoming absolutely still and falling into a deep sleep. If I could find a dark place soon enough, and drop into a deep enough sleep, the headache might last only a few hours - if not, it could be there for days.

When I was fifteen, the headaches had gotten so bad that my mother took me to specialists to find out if I had a brain tumor. After extended testing that found no physical answers, I was sent to the psychiatric unit of a major teaching hospital where I was interviewed in front of an auditorium of doctors. I remember the interviewer asking me questions about my siblings and about a bone growth in my chest that had been discovered. The interviewing psychiatrist announced to the audience of interns that this was a typical case of sibling rivalry in which I was having headaches to get attention. He recommended psychiatric counseling to my mother who was devastated by the whole experience, and we were dismissed. My headaches were never mentioned again. Counseling was out of the question as far as my parents were concerned. I learned to have headaches without letting any one know that I was having them.

I spent twenty-three years in a marriage where sexual activity was silently dreaded and pain related to orgasm was so intense that my body became limp and numb to avoid experiencing feelings. I was frigid and didn't know what to do, so I pretended not to be. I, like many other women who were sexually abused as children, struggled with weight from puberty onward.

Unsuccessful struggles through countless diets left me discouraged and highly self-critical. After losing sixty pounds in my thirties, and reclaiming my high school figure, I went through a period of bulimia followed by anorexia. A few years later I regained the weight I had lost. . . and gained even more.

Seeking Help and Discovering Pain

In 1986, personal, traumatic events in my life related to my marriage caused me to decide that life was too painful to continue and I planned to end my life in suicide. In one last effort to find help, I went to a therapist. This began what was to be a four-year journey into a hidden, inner world that held the memories that I didn't know how to handle when they first erupted into my conscious awareness. Three therapists, David, Michael, and Steven helped me to unearth the causes of physical, mental and spiritual illness. I had opened the inner spaces, walked the hallways and entered the rooms where frightened, separated parts of myself had hidden for decades. Many had shown me the events that had sent them into their own darkness, and as they did, I experienced body responses as memories returned from some thirty or forty years before.

One of the most distressing body responses occurred in the fall of 1989 near the end of the four-year period I was in therapy. For quite some time, I had maintained a pattern of waiting until midnight or later to take my dog on her walk. That way, I could be sure that I would not have to see people if I took her out after almost everyone had gone to bed. I began to feel panic with those night walks, a panic that began when she tugged at her chain to go faster. Her pulls caused me to walk more quickly, and I had to run to keep her from choking herself. As my feet hit the mud-packed earth, I heard the cries of a child in my head. Each night I saw the same flash memory that had come back much earlier in my therapy work, a memory I thought I had healed some time before.

Early in my therapy, the memory of this event first came back to me just as a feeling of terror related to being in some confined and dark place. As I worked with that feeling-memory, I realized that there was a crack in the darkness through which I could see a shovel, which was dropping dirt on me. At first all I could see was the shovel, then I could see the hand that was on the shovel, and then I saw my father's face. It was excruciatingly painful when I knew that my father had buried me alive.

The memory had come back in tiny pieces over several months like little puzzle parts that finally came together in one horrible realization. After being raped at age four, I told my mother that my father had hurt me "down there." My mother confronted him and he denied it, and then my father punished me for "lying" by tying me up, putting me in a box, and burying the box in the ground. I could see him through a tiny crack between the wood slats when another shovel-full of dirt hit one of the slats and broke it causing dirt to fall into my face. I couldn't move my hands to clear the dirt that covered my nose and mouth. In my work with this memory, I removed the child from the box and brought her to a healing pond where she was cleaned and made whole. I didn't know there was still more to do.

On that late night walk in 1989, I felt a stabbing pain in my leg that was related to that burial event from 40 years before. The sharp pain somehow opened the place within me where I held the memory of what happened after my father buried me in the box. Within a few hours of that sharp piercing feeling in my leg, a small blister appeared on my right shin about half way between my ankle and knee. The blister broke and a hole began to open up. In the next few days the hole grew to the size of a dime and then a quarter and soon the pain was so great I could not walk. I went to several specialists. One said the damage might have been caused by a recluse spider bite and if that was the case, I might lose my leg if we could not stop the wound from growing larger. He recommended a few more days of observation before scheduling surgery to remove the surrounding tissue to prevent more muscle damage. Although the wound was open to the bone, there was no infection and no visible cause.

Each doctor removed the packing material that the previous doctor had used to fill the hole, and looked at the wound. The tissue had not turned black, as it would have if it had been a spider bite, and no one knew how to diagnose this growing hole in my leg. I had to move around on crutches and was warned to walk as little as possible as the hole opened to half-dollar size. I mentioned the memory of the box and the pain in that very place in my leg, but none of the specialists took it seriously.

While still fumbling around on crutches, I took my dog out for another night walk, when I remembered that forty years before when I was buried in that box and the slat broke, a nail, or perhaps a staple pierced my right leg. I experienced the terror of my child-self when she could feel that there was not enough air to breathe and dirt was falling into her nose and mouth. A chain of terrifying thoughts occurred to the little girl that if she made no sound maybe her daddy would dig her out and she would be ok, but it was possible that if she made no sound, he would forget she was there and she would die. But then, if she made a sound he might become angrier and leave her there. When I was just four years old I made my lungs get smaller and I dropped into inner darkness and silence and begged God to let me come home.

I don't know how long I was in the box or how I got out of the box. But I remember that Mamma was laughing and telling me that it was only a joke as she cleaned dirt from my mouth and nose. Daddy grabbed my arms at the wrists and began pulling me toward an old wood storage shed that had a dirt floor. A piercing pain shot though my leg as he dragged me behind him into the shed but I couldn't say anything. He punished me again but this time as he violently sodomized me, my father warned me never to tell anyone ever again. I obeyed that warning for forty years.

In 1989, when my dog pulled on the chain causing both my hands to feel the tugging and my feet to make a slapping sound against the ground, it matched the feeling in my body of being pulled by my father toward the shed. And I remembered what I had not remembered before. The body memory of the staple hole in my leg contained not only the pain of the staple penetrating my leg, but also the pain caused by the wound as I was being pulled into the shed. The body memory contained the fear of what was going to happen, the agonizing horror of the anal rape, and the terrifying warning never to speak of what had happened. Though I had recalled the box earlier in my therapy, until that night that I was being pulled by my puppy, I had not remembered the nail, the pain in my leg and the horror of what followed. After the full memory came back in an excruciatingly painful abreaction, my leg healed quickly leaving a scar that looks as if it was made by a staple.

In those four years, from early 1986 to late 1989, everything in my life had fallen apart; everything had collapsed. My belief system had crumbled and my sense of self was obliterated. It was as if all of my foundations and structures had been shattered. Through the cracks and broken pieces, the memories of my childhood years continued to leak through. The event when I was four was just the beginning. This time of memory leakage was an exhausting period. At the end of the fourth year, with what seemed to be a majority of the memories retrieved, I finalized my divorce and decided to take time out from the inner journey of therapy to begin another journey; this one was in the outer world, to China.

For nearly two years I lived in the center of the People's Republic of China, in the Baoji district of Shaanxi Province where I was the only foreigner among three million Chinese. I taught English in Baoji Teachers' College and worked in a Qi Gong medical clinic learning about Chinese diagnosis and healing methods. Absolutely everything in my life was new. No sights, no sounds, no tastes, no language, no life patterns, nothing that touched any of my senses was familiar. With everything coming in from the outside being unfamiliar, I had to create a whole new construct of the world. It was exactly what I needed to withdraw from the world of my former life and re-group. It was there that I could reconstruct foundations; I could look at the world and see it in a much clearer way without old connotations or interpretations. In some ways it was like being born again, but as an adult instead of as an infant. It was in China that I deeply re-connected with my essence and my spiritual knowing. I discovered that I was neither my trauma nor my story. I discovered simply that I am.

In the late fall of 1991, I returned to America, taught in a Junior College in Florida for a few months, and then went to New Zealand to study to be trained as a clinical hypnotherapist. I wrote what I believed was the completed story of my struggle toward healing, which was a 261-page manuscript that covered the events of my life up to that time. I thought it was clear and could be published. I titled that work *Melting the Chains* and sent it out to agents and publishers. I was both devastated and relieved that it was rejected. Though it contained a great deal of information, the chains had not yet been melted; the story was neither integrated nor complete. Within the pages, there were many more puzzle pieces that needed to be connected to make sense of a still scattered and shattered life.

I had written *Melting the Chains* partially to be understood, but also to understand for myself what had happened to me. My life had changed so dramatically and it seemed as if I did not know the San Dy of the past. It was as if a curtain had dropped and whoever I had been on the other side of that curtain, no longer existed. I wanted to piece together whatever I knew about the "me" on the other side to try to better understand "me" that was on this side.

The San Dy on the Back Side of the Curtain

San Dy's life before sixteen was one of bits and pieces, snatches here and there of memories shared by her family of seven. But in some ways, who she was in the world began when she was a junior in high school. At that time she had met John, a quiet boy in her class, and a short time later, she had promised to marry him. He had endeared himself to her at Christmas by buying her an electric blanket to keep her warm and fend off a persistent cough. No one had ever given her such a special gift before. When she graduated from high school, she and John were unofficially engaged.

When she was nineteen John became angry that his girlfriend had been given a pelvic exam during a mandatory physical that was required when she made a college transfer between her freshman and sophomore years. He expressed a belief that he had been betrayed because another man had seen her naked before he did. He became jealous and attempted to rape her. He apologized and begged her to not leave him, and though she stayed, she never felt safe again.

San Dy's fundamentalist Christian upbringing caused her to hold firmly to the standard of not having intercourse before marriage, but her boyfriend's equally strong desire to be sexual placed her in constant defense and compromise. After John had accused her of betraying him by having a doctor see her for the pelvic examination, but before her marriage, she compromised her own beliefs and allowed John to see her naked to make up for her betrayal. For years she struggled with unrelenting guilt, believing that she had betrayed her faith by having made that compromise.

San Dy came from a financially unstable family; she owed thousands of dollars from college loans; she had no income and no dowry at the time of her marriage. The only gift she had to offer John was her virginity. Though she had no reason to believe that she didn't want to marry John, San Dy was oppressed by a dream that seemed to be a warning about marriage. Each time she had the dream, she awoke in turmoil and then pushed it away. John had seen her naked, and she had made a commitment; she was obligated to be married. She was married at twenty-one, a month after her college graduation in 1966. Though San Dy had compassion for John, she didn't know if she loved him at the time of her marriage; however, if anyone had asked her if she did, she would have answered with absolute certainty that she loved him.

Not long after she was married, San Dy's father shocked everyone by leaving her mother to live with a woman with whom he had a child. A few months after that shattering departure, John was drafted into the army and was eventually sent to Vietnam. While her husband was in the war zone, San Dy lived with her mother and did substitute teaching. Instead of taking the offer to live with John's parents who would have provided well for her, San Dy decided to stay with her mother to keep her from being lonely and depressed. The decision to be with her mother meant staying in a house that had been nearly destroyed by fire two years before and still smelled of acrid smoke, a house without heating in the cold Northwest winters, a house that had but one livable room.

During that year she and her mother lived in the dining room that served also as bedroom and living room. The room was heated by a small plug-in heater that they could not keep on too long at a time because of the cost of electricity. Blankets were nailed to the door leading to the kitchen and to the opening that led to the living room to keep heat contained in the small space. San Dy slept in the bed at night and her mother who worked as a night nurse slept in the bed during the day. Her only respite that first winter were the days she was asked to do substitute teaching, earning enough to help out her mother and to save for the day when John would come home.

San Dy counted the days until John's return. She wanted him back but she dreaded what that would mean. There were so many double feelings that reminded her of the nights during that first year of marriage when John often came home very late from work. He didn't like her calling him at his office, but he wouldn't let her know when he was staying late into the night. So many nights she went to bed waiting for the sound of a creak from the front door opening and footsteps across the living room floor. In the silence of those nights she waited with anxious anticipation. And then she would hear the key in the door. She would sigh - a sigh of relief that he was home safe - but in the sound of her sigh was sadness that there would be another night, another day when she had to struggle with unbearable feelings that had underneath them wishes he would not come home.

After his return from Vietnam, the harder she tried to please him, the more critical he became. Devastated by his treatment, by October of 1976, she built up the courage to ask him what was wrong. He denied that there was a problem. A few days later San Dy finally told him she was thinking of leaving him. For the first time she spoke from a place of power and stated that if he left for work without talking, she would not be there when he returned. He stayed a short time; they talked. He told her he didn't know what love was and wanted to move out on his own. He assured her that there was not another woman.

San Dy listened to him with surprising calmness and helped him move to a nearby city; she helped him pick out a bedroom set and furnishings for his new place. He moved out on Halloween night, ten years after they had married. She fell apart after he left and wanted to die but somehow she went on as if nothing happened. She didn't speak of his leaving to anyone. Sometime later he returned, never saying why he left or why he came back. She didn't ask.

Soon John became discouraged with his career and eventually quit to start a business of his own. San Dy supported him for two years with her income from teaching while he struggled to find his way into private enterprise. He was a proud traditionalist, which made this time difficult for both of them. Eventually, a business began to grow. It was a low-margin business but provided needed income. He buried himself in his work and became increasingly separate from her. There was seldom a sense of closeness; there were simply degrees of distance.

San Dy continued teaching until 1979, leaving the profession because her heart was not focused on her work any more. She considered taking a job in Washington, D. C., to see if *absence really would make the heart grow fonder,* but that didn't work out. While trying to find herself, San Dy began a small enterprise of her own under the financial wing of her husband's business. She began selling products for commercial projects. It was a much higher profit-margin business than the business that John had built, but in the beginning stages it had a much lower volume. In a couple of years, her business began to out-produce his and John took over her part of the enterprise and eventually San Dy became a non-paid employee. She accepted his decision that they must put everything back into the company for it to grow and was an obedient wife; however, a sense of injustice began to arise inside her.

San Dy began to commit more of her time to a politically focused foundation and eventually accepted a part-time position in the foundation, which required travel to Washington D. C. several times a year. Part of her responsibilities included writing speeches for political leaders and coordinating statewide, regional, and national conferences. San Dy split her attention between this job and her work with John.

When she was home, business often occupied seven days a week, twelve or more hours a day. As she became more of a public figure, John became more critical of the time she spent away from the business. She enjoyed the respect that was given to her in this new-paid position, unlike the verbal and psychological abuse that she was receiving at home and at the office from John.

John continually expressed his unhappiness with San Dy. He was dissatisfied with her as a housewife. He often told her that it was a good thing he married her because no one else would have. He didn't remember her birthday, or Valentines Day, or other holidays. He mocked her increasing weight. Whatever self-esteem she had was becoming more and more eroded. She tried so many times, so many ways to lose weight unsuccessfully. He attempted to sabotage her weight loss by offering her fattening foods and when she did lose weight, he became more abusive and publicly critical. San Dy felt as if he was trying to push her out of his life. At one point he told her that she was not a virgin when he married her because she had been fitted for a diaphragm before their marriage. She was devastated. He had shredded the value of the only gift she believed she had given him at the beginning of their marriage.

San Dy began to suspect that her husband was involved with a woman with whom he had business dealings. She later discovered that he had been in an ongoing relationship with her for a number of years beginning when he left San Dy years before on Halloween. Between a series of relationships intended to take the place of John, the woman would reappear for consolation and reintroduce the idea of leaving San Dy for her. During these times, San Dy's husband became more abusive. His degree of distance was directly related to his connection with the woman. His own infidelity led to his attack on San Dy's virginity. He used the opportunity of her Washington trips to meet with his lover. Each time San Dy traveled to the nation's capitol, she hoped that John would ask her where she was staying and wished he would surprise her with a call, but he never did. By the end of 1984, San Dy was more lonely than she would have been if she had no husband.

While in Washington, San Dy did not socialize with foundation people until a trip she took in April of 1985. A group of Canadian participants invited her to join them for an evening after a political dinner. One of the men spent a great deal of the evening talking with her about everything from politics to favorite movies. John had never asked her about her opinions. John had never indicated that he cared about her feelings as this man did. For the first time she shared her inner life with another person. They had only that one evening of conversation that included an unexpected good-night kiss, but when each returned to their own homes, they began a loving correspondence and she kept his letters in a large foundation envelope in her desk at work.

In December of 1985, the man invited San Dy to visit him in Canada. Someone inside of her that San Dy didn't even know agreed to go see him following a foundation meeting and she found herself on a plane from Washington, D.C. to Toronto. She had no idea what caused her to challenge her lifetime beliefs and risk her twenty-year marriage to meet a man whom she only knew through letters. San Dy was terrified of what she was doing but felt deeply happy. She was about to be with the man she had fallen in love with through months of correspondence. They spent two days together, and though he wanted to make love, she could not let herself do it. She knew that if she did, she would be ending her marriage.

She boarded the plane waving good-bye through the falling pre-Christmas snow, and never saw him again. There were times she wondered what it would have been like to be able to make love with someone she truly loved and who loved her. She returned to Washington, D. C. and then went back to the Northwest. San Dy wondered if she would be condemned to die for what she had done.

For the next two months these two lonely people wrote almost daily. She had a large collection of tender, loving letters in her desk drawer, a hidden reminder that someone very far away cared for her. In mid February of 1986, San Dy went to her desk to put another letter in the envelope and it was missing. Fearing the worst she went into a panic. There was no evidence that anyone had the envelope, but she could not live with the fear. She could not bear to see the disappointment on her husband's face if he were to discover that she had become involved with another man. Even though the involvement was primarily through letters, she felt in her heart that she had betrayed the man for whom she had vowed to forsake all others.

San Dy condemned herself for never having made her husband happy. She cursed herself for bringing potential trouble to her Canadian friend who was also married. She decided that the only solution for her unforgivable sin was to end her life. The large insurance policy she had on her life would give her husband the one thing she knew would really make him happy, which was a 46-foot cruiser that he could buy with the insurance money. She carefully planned her drowning to take place on the next extended outing on their 32-foot boat. She believed it was the most logical way to handle the impossible situation if she could not find the envelope, destroy it, contact her Canadian friend to end the relationship, and never experience such passion again.

San Dy made an appointment with David, a psychologist she found who was also a hypnotherapist. She told him she wanted to have him hypnotize her so she could find what she did with the envelope. However, during the first session, David insisted on asking her irrelevant questions, like, what was in the envelope, and was she happy, and finally what would happen if the envelope were to be found by someone else. San Dy broke down and sobbed, "If John finds it, I will have to die."

David worked with San Dy for three more years. Shortly after the loss of the letters, the Canadian man withdrew from the relationship. She was in agony over having lost her only connection with feeling loved, yet she hated herself for making it impossible to find love in her relationship with John. While on the next trip to Washington, D. C., San Dy met another man. He was a kind man, an Atlanta high school principal who was separated from his wife and trying to find a new life for himself. He let her look into his eyes and when she did, San Dy saw compassion and love. They began to write after her return. As in the previous relationship, this man also opened his heart to her. After a few months, he invited her on a vacation with him to Sarasota, Florida; she agreed, as long as it was non-sexual. He accepted, and kept his promise.

When San Dy returned home, things began to happen that she could not explain. She found partially written letters, open and exposed on her desk, in the office she shared with John. The letters were to her friend in Atlanta. San Dy nearly went into shock one afternoon when she returned from a business lunch to find a picture of her Canadian friend out in the open. The photo was on her desk propped up against the wall. Another time that same picture was in full view on the dashboard of John's car, which was parked in their garage at home. No one else had access to her letters or to the picture, which she knew she had not put in those places. She thought she was going insane.

Headaches became prominent; something had gone very wrong. Her world was falling apart. One of her company employees discovered a letter that was left on another desk in the office and confronted her with it, threatening to tell John. She became frantic but decided to tell him herself. Her heart pounded in the silence of her bedroom as she waited for John to come home. As he came up the stairs to the master suite, she whispered she had something very difficult to tell him and wanted to know if he loved her. He responded that he didn't want to talk right then. . . and then asked her if maybe she pretended that everything was ok today, and then did it again the next day and again the next that maybe in a few days it would really be ok. He seemed to have sensed that she was going to tell him what he didn't want to hear. He left the room and they never talked.

The final blow came when San Dy began a relationship with a local man. A high school reunion was taking place in the summer of 1986 and San Dy wanted to go. She asked John to go with her. Perhaps there was a chance that in the old crowd and reconnected with the memories of the past, she could recapture the feelings that used to be there for the young man who brought her the electric blanket on that cold winter night so many years before. John refused to go, so San Dy went without him.

While at the reunion, San Dy met a man she had first known when they were both in junior high. She remembered him immediately as the boy who sat in the base section in the high school choir. They spent the evening talking of old times and mutual friends. Though both of them acknowledged that they were not interested in a romantic relationship, they acknowledged that they were open for a friendship.

Over the months the relationship flourished. She had discovered love in the eyes of a third man. Her conditions for the relationship were the same as those with the Canadian and the Georgian, loving friendship without sexuality. San Dy found time to spend with him whenever she could and felt cared for. She met him at restaurants and occasionally went to his home for lunch or dinner.

And then one day, or perhaps it was an evening, something happened. She was sitting with this man on his couch and he began to kiss her. She could not remember how she had gotten to his house or how the event happened. All she could remember is falling into a black hole. She woke in his bed with him rocking her, touching her face and calling her name. He was terrified. Apparently she had been unconscious from the time the kissing led to foreplay and the beginning attempt at intercourse. He had promised no intercourse but broke the promise. She believed she was forever ruined and wanted to die, but she had no idea how she had gotten into such a life-threatening situation.

Suicide and her sometimes on, sometimes off relationship with her husband were prominent throughout the remainder of her therapy with David. The sexual incident with the man had precipitated flashback memories of rape that began to emerge uncontrollably into San Dy's consciousness.

San Dy's internal system was in chaos, matching the chaos of her outer world. She had lost control of the inner structure of herself and frightened parts of herself frantically struggled to regain order, creating violent internal wars, increased memory loss, and headaches that left her incapacitated. She could not explain what had caused her to commit such horrible sins that condemned her to Hell forever. She felt as if she had no one to turn to, not even God. She didn't know what had happened to the quiet submissive wife who promised to stand by her husband, to be faithful and to grow old with him. What had happened to the schoolteacher who dressed in conservative brown and tan and taught Sunday school in her husband's church? San Dy didn't know the woman who was taking over her life, nor did she understand where the horrible thoughts and pictures were coming from that were invading her head. None of the pictures had happened to her; there was no acceptable explanation for how they got there, but they invaded her days and her nights. There was no peace.

After three years, her first therapist moved to another state and San Dy found another. For a year he sat with her as she re-experienced atrocities that had caused massive splitting in her child-self. She was violently raped by her father at age four and buried alive in a box as punishment for telling her mother what he had done. While still in grade school she was prostituted to her father's associates and used in unspeakable ways. Her mother was a fundamentalist Christian who taught her that she was a vile creature, black of heart, evil, and as unacceptable as filthy rags. She feared the end times and the coming of the Lord when he would destroy all that was evil, including her. She spent her life trying to prove to God that she was not bad but underneath she believed that there was no hope for her wretched soul. And the terrible sin she had committed with the third man was proof of how wretched she was.

By the time she was working with her second therapist, she was living alone and had cut off all outside relationships. Though separated with divorce papers filed, she was not divorced. Her days and nights were spent responding to abreactions that were exhausting and painful. Rapes were relived in her adult body as if they had just happened. For days after a rape memory returned, and there were many such incidents from her childhood, walking was difficult if not impossible. Sights of torture were imprinted on her body, and she felt the pain. She experienced claustrophobia and agoraphobia simultaneously. Life felt intolerable. At one point the seeming impossibility of healing caused her to shut her system down as she had done at four when she was buried in the box, coming very close to dying. However, a telephone call from her sister in the "adult shut-down attempt" revived her within moments of the total closing of her system.

After about a year or so in therapy, San Dy had a dream that caused her to believe that she would be going to China. The dream began to grow in her thoughts and finally after four years of intense inner work, she decided to follow her dream. It seemed that most of the memories had been retrieved. She needed a break time to heal. She made the decision to end her therapy, her relationships, and her life the way she had been living it and moved to China where she lived for almost two years.

San Dy went through many changes in China. She learned to see the world and herself, in a whole new way. She returned to the States in the fall of 1991 prepared to begin life over again. Somewhere between Japan and mainland U.S.A., San Dy decided that she had become strong enough to re-enter her relationship with John and make it work. When he picked her up at the airport, she found out that he was getting married the next weekend. San Dy felt a shock flow through her. She felt two feelings, heart-breaking sadness and tremendous relief.

San Dy accepted a job offer in Florida that same day. She left to begin a new life teaching and working with mid-life women who were re-entering college as students. She was back in the United States, but as far away from John and from her family as she could be and still be in her homeland. A few months after settling into her new home in Florida, she mustered the courage to write a letter to her family telling them about her life and the pain of her childhood. Her mother responded with a letter expressing shock that San Dy could believe such lies and condemned therapists who would cause children to believe such horrible things about parents. San Dy then began to write about her life, which resulted in a manuscript, *Melting the Chains*, in which she told the story of the scattering and shattering of her life. She sent the manuscript to a few publishers and it was rejected - which was both discouraging and relieving.

Another New Beginning

The San Dy who wrote the manuscript did the best she could. Her work was not finished, though she thought it was. This San Dy was but one of the many alters who made up my whole self. She was the last of a long list of alter personalities, who had taken on the responsibility of being what therapists refer to as *host*. After the original split when I was a very small child, I seemed to have formed a quadrant system of four parts that were in charge and shifted hosting responsibilities depending on the circumstances. When one part, identified as Jenny, who was deeply distressed by loneliness took over in 1985 without consent of the other three, leadership was shattered, causing a period of chaos. This 1985-1986 insurgent host took charge when she met the Canadian and finally experienced a relationship with someone who seemed to love her. However, she had faltered in her responsibility to seek a loving relationship, when the man she had known in high school broke his promise. That failure led to the major burn-down of the former internal system and eventually ended the life I had lived for 23 years.

The host who had risen from the ashes after the major internal fire was that part of me who decided to see a therapist in 1986, to seek a divorce, to move to China in 1990, and to find help in February of 1993 when I contacted Dr. Ben Keyes. She was the one who helped me begin the sixteen-month process of integrating my broken self. My pre-China therapeutic work had centered on memory retrieval of the causes of multiplicity and splintering. The new work that was in front of me in 1993 was to piece together a lifetime of scattered parts of self and out of many parts to recreate one whole self.

The first sessions were taken up with filling Ben in on my past and attempting to find a way to approach a feeling that pulsed somewhere in the center of me that kept screaming to get out. It seemed to be there all the time. That part of me felt frightened and lost, and did not know how to find the way out of the space in which it was trapped. And the host San Dy did not know how to find her way in.

During one of the sessions in early 1993, Ben asked me to go inside to the "safe place" where I could meet the child part, with whom we had been working. My safe place was in a large open field. Near the end of the hour, Ben asked if there were any others who would come and join us in the field. As I looked around, I saw myriad children in scattered places. Ben asked if I would be willing to draw what I was seeing. That night, I began my first drawing.

I rolled out a piece of poster paper on my glass dining table and stared at it... white paper... empty... Without forethought, I picked up a colored pen and began to draw. First, a long thin stone building began to form in the far-left corner. As I drew it, my chest felt crushed and oppressed. Then a building in the far right corner took form. I could feel the howl sounds on the inside as I drew the second structure. I didn't like drawing that building with the orange-red fire around it, because it felt as if the drawing was coming alive. Each pen stroke seemed to be revealing what was already there. There was a hopelessness that filled me when the black wrought iron fence with no gate grew up around what seemed to be some sort of a compound. Three chained people appeared on the outside of the building. I had no idea who they were. The foreground began to fill in.

With each child I drew, I could feel anguish though I had no idea where the pain was coming from. It seemed silly that a drawing could have such power. Rows and rows of rocks appeared with children hidden behind the rocks. They were the hollow people who filled and frightened me. A woman stood in the foreground with blood flowing from her heart and her side. She seemed to be in anguish. I didn't know what to do for her. The drawing was complete.

I brought the finished product to Ben, and as he unrolled it, I told him I didn't think it meant anything; but as he studied it, his expression told me I was wrong. A couple of weeks later, in the middle of the night, I was awakened with a horrible pain in my side. A few hours later I was in the hospital having an emergency appendix operation. I saw flashes of the drawing and the woman in the foreground with blood flowing from her side while I was lying on the operating table. I wondered about the meaning of this. There was a stream of blood flowing from the woman's heart in what looked like two traumas; one was lighter and the other was darker. (In 1996 and again in 2001, I was in the hospital after having experienced heart attacks. Not until my editing of this writing in 2003 did I notice the stream of blood flowing from my vaginal area in the drawing. And as I write these words, I am working with my body to heal a severe stage-three dysplasia condition on my cervix).

Over the next few months, the work with Ben continued as before but somehow during each session I would see a flash of one of the children in the grassy field. The work we were doing was connected to the drawing though I wasn't sure how. It was later that I discovered that this drawing had been predictive of the work we did in therapy. What I drew became the map for the next few weeks to months of therapy. After the final integration was completed and the maps were assembled, Ben and I discovered that therapy followed the drawings in a circular pattern in a clockwise direction, from outside to inside, in a spiral, just as I had drawn them.

A couple of months after the first drawing, Ben asked me to draw another picture. He told me it didn't have to look like the first one; it could be anything I wanted. I had intended to ask him for the original drawing that he had kept in his office but forgot. I was left with just letting the drawing happen. Again, as in the previous drawing, I found myself becoming absorbed by the pictures that were appearing on this second sheet of poster paper. The map took a couple of days to complete. The last time, the blue rock-compound was drawn first. This time the blackened prison was what flowed from the colored pens first. I noticed my chest hurt and I felt like crying while it was being drawn. There were two levels and two sides on the inside of the prison.

As I was drawing, I found myself inside the building telling the ones who lived within the walls that they could have windows and soft feather beds if they wanted. Some of the children wanted windows and curtains. Others put shades over their windows. Some made the windows black, not wanting to see or be seen by the outside. I told them they could change the windows whenever they wanted. The interior of the prison was a dark yellow-brown color like an old faded movie, scorched by too many showings. Most of the residents in the thirty-six-cell prison did not feel comfortable being seen. I didn't stay or try to force a meeting. It seemed I had been in this prison-house before with David just before he moved away.

I tried to put three chained ones outside as I recalled having them in the last drawing but only two came. I don't know what happened to the third. I also noticed that another entrance appeared, guarded by two people, one blue, the other, red. The blue one seemed to want to be sure that anyone who passed did so without judgment. She wanted only pure souls to pass. The red one was trying to frighten anyone who wanted to enter this unholy place. My first response was not to like the red one very much. There appeared a connection between the little ones and the back entrance to the prison. Next, a cross just appeared on the page. Then someone was on it and the cross became a chained necklace that turned into a marker for the Bible.

The group of five on the lower right appeared next. They seemed oblivious to the rest of the picture. They formed an inner circle and together were responsible for dealing with the outside world. These were the first "alters" that I had met while working with David. Peggy was at the high noon place. She was my organizer part, the one who got me through school, who taught my classes, who wrote speeches for Senators and Governors, and who was asked to run for the State legislature. She organized a Pacific-rim economic conference in San Francisco, choreographed a nationally televised teleconference with former U. N. Ambassador Kilpatrick, and developed a successful business.

Jenny, at six o'clock was the untouched feminine part. She was in love with love and saw something good in everything. She was the one who wanted to be free from a loveless marriage and caused the inner system to collapse. Jennifer and Yvonne were at three o'clock. They were the carriers of depression and fear, and often wanted to die; they were always on alert, watching for anything that looked questionable. Martha was at nine o'clock. It was her job to hold to the traditions. She was the obedient daughter, the loyal wife. As long as there was no major threat, this group worked together and controlled the outer shell of the person known as San Dy.

I am not sure what happened to the ones from the hollow who hid behind the rocks that had been in the first drawing. Several layers were just not there anymore. I began to recognize specific incidents that appeared to be reflected by figures in the drawing. When each appeared on the paper, my body reflected the pain, the sadness, the terror, and the hopelessness of whatever part I was drawing. As I continued, I seemed to drop deeper into a state in which the drawing seemed to draw itself.

The path to the jail separated and fire grew up from deep beneath the ground. It had black tornadoes coming out of it like the tornado of blackness growing above the child with eight people around her. It also matched the tornado that sucked me into the deep well when the black spot came to the top of my head. That black spot always came in the form of a devastating headache that pulled whoever was out, back to the deep inside. Eventually I learned that there was some new information coming from some hidden part of me.

The two people who floated above everything in the last drawing turned into three and they seem to have created an energy force around them at the top center. This was related to the hope I had been feeling since the last drawing, a hope that was growing within me in spite of the hopelessness I was also feeling. It was also related to trust that seemed to be increasing in spite of the fact I still didn't know how to trust and to a developing sense of love when my world seemed devoid of love.

The blue compound, where the wounded children lived, appeared to be more open, covered with green ivy. A mountain became visible and a waterfall that led to a beautiful pond and garden, not visible in the drawing, took form. There were many rooms inside this compound. Stronger children guarded the wounded children behind the stone walls. Many of the fragile ones were unable to move and wanted to leave the Earth if they could find a way. As I drew, I could hear the pleading sounds of their voices asking God to let them come home. I felt a weakness come over me as I drew the blue compound. I wanted to die.

As I watched the three figures appear in the foreground, I knew that they were central to the drawing though I didn't know how. One believed that she was chained and trapped forever, that things would never be different. The other knew no chains. She was connected to a spiritual world unaffected by the traumas. The one in the middle had to disconnect from the ones on either side.

Though I was distressed at not having the other map so I would not make a mistake about where things needed to go, I decided to accept what had been created even if it didn't match the first drawing. When I was finished, I stood in front of the large sheet. I allowed my right hand to float over the surface and felt emotions flow through me uncontrollably. When I brought this drawing in to my next session, Ben studied the completed work and pointed out changes that I had not noticed.

A few weeks later I had dropped into a particularly dark place and decided to draw another map. With another large piece of poster paper on my table, I stared into the emptiness and felt hopeless. There was a silent ache in the center of my chest that howl-cried for a voice that was not available to it. I tried to draw something. . . Perhaps if I drew the light blue compound at the top left hand side. . . But I couldn't make pictures come. Instead, I felt myself falling into a tornado and heard voices coming from the walls of the vortex. I wrote the words of the voices as I dropped past them. As the words appeared on the paper, I became the ones who spoke the words.

The damaged children from the left side of the paper had gone to God and begged him to let them come home but instead they were sent to the blue compound. I felt their cell-level disappointment at having to stay in this world and wrote their words. I felt the plight, the hopelessness reflected in the ones who believed no one was there to hear, or care, the ones who believed they did not exist. I was frightened by the ones who hated me and judged me, and I ached when I felt the part who believed God hated me.

My sense of desperation, of being trapped with no way out and no way to let God know how scared I was, caused me to drop into the blackness. Voices of condemnation and other voices of defense ended with a plea for sleep. I felt drained from the experience of drawing the tornado and writing the voices. I went to sleep with a black headache.

In my next session with Ben, I brought the tornado poster, telling him I was sorry it wasn't a picture so perhaps it might not be useful to him in our work. Ben studied my presentation and helped me to see that the large pictures had collapsed into this drawing with seventeen voices. Progress had in fact occurred and was represented in my newest work. Sessions that followed in the next few weeks appeared to involve addressing the parts of me caught in the whirlwind. It was later that I discovered the tornado had appeared in my earlier drawing.

Drawings continued throughout my therapeutic experience, each one reflecting the integration process that had occurred up to that point or predicting the next arenas of our work. Some depicted the way my body was feeling at the time. These later drawings were connected to memories or events that had not yet emerged into my consciousness.

The expanded left, right, and center places of the original two drawings had congealed into three major parts of self, by now identified as San Dy, Sela and Sara. San Dy, my mental self, the one I identified myself with at the time, had the responsibility of dealing with the outside world. San Dy was a compilation of Peggy, Jenny, Martha, Jennifer and Yvonne in their "thinking" roles. The "feelings" parts of these four were within Sara.

Sara carried all the memories in the body. She was my physical self. Sara contained Bonnie who had been buried in a box as punishment for saying that her daddy was the one who hurt her "down there." Sara held the memories of the extreme abuse and also contained the almost eight-year-old who attempted suicide looking for the only way out of the intolerable childhood.

Sela had the connection with the Angels; she held my spiritual knowing. It was Sela who worked with clients who came for therapy in my clinical practice in the early years, and Sela was the one who could braid together the experiences of Sara and the learning of San Dy. These three also appeared in the previous drawings, but now were fully clear.

In February of 1994, a drawing showed Sela on the left, San Dy in the center comforting two children, one on the left carrying seven flowers and crying, and Sara seated on a rock with two children next to the rock and a dark figure in the background. Sara did not want to look at anything, especially the dark figure on her right. If she did, she was afraid she would fall into the blackness and die without dying... feeling the icy fire and being forever lost. Yvonne, a part of Sara, believed she was already lost. Many weeks were spent with Sara in therapy. When I asked the dark figure if it would let itself be drawn, I discovered a child underneath.

May 17, 1994 another drawing was completed. Sara, Sela and San Dy seemed so close. I decided to ask Sela to draw the three of us as she experienced us. We three were connected at arm's length and Sela had loving guides around her. San Dy drew the three of us with San Dy in the middle, Sara being comforted in San Dy's arms, and Sela embracing both. Sara drew Sela and San Dy holding hands and drew herself curled up and isolated. When I looked at Sela and Sara's drawings I knew Sara felt disconnected and afraid. I asked her to show me why she felt so alone. She drew Sela as one connected to Spirit, rainbows and infinity; San Dy was connected with life and the future. But Sara... Sara was connected with the horror of the past. She believed she was condemned because she was physical, because she was mortal, and because she held the horrors of the past experiences. She drew the awful things that made it impossible for her to connect with the others. She felt hopeless.

Sela communicated most beautifully to Sara, telling her that Sara was truly significant; she told her that the physical was the visible expression of beliefs of the emotional and mental self. Only when hidden beliefs could be manifested, would there be any hope for transformation. Sara had an integral part to play in the healing of my divided self. Sara reached out to me and accepted my embrace. She wept.

For several days San Dy had been resisting integration, fearing that Sara would somehow pollute Sela if the two came together. A session with my Florida body therapist, another David, brought back the body memory of being tied in a chair with a strap tightly wrapped around my head. There were wires running from the strap to a box. I felt horrible jolts entering my head that filled my body. Someone was sending electrical impulses into my head. I felt the shocks as David worked with me. Each one sent my heart and my body into fibrillation.

As the memory returned in full, I could see the arcs of electricity on the inside of my body splitting and twisting my own internal energy flow. It was as if the foreign electrical shocks had splintered my energy system to the point where my energy system could not recognize what was San Dy and what was not San Dy. My inner communication had been severed. As David helped me release the foreign energy, my own system reconnected. It was like a magnificent homecoming. The enemy had been removed and all that was left was ally. It seemed that spontaneous integration was in process when I visualized the safe place and saw all the children who made up Sela stand on the left side in a clearing and all the children who made up Sara on the right. They began to form into two parallel lines as if they were twins. Pair by pair they began to come together as a zipper connecting left to right, somehow joining and then merging into the pair in front until there was just Sela and Sara on either side, with San Dy in between.

A fear filled the "me" that was San Dy that something bad would happen if I let the integration complete itself. I refused to let it continue. The next day in session, I told Ben about the experience. He assured me that it was not possible to pollute Sela. In that moment, I knew he was right. Ben asked me to go to the safe place. Sela was standing in the same clearing watching the children play. She said she enjoyed watching them, but would be willing to call them all home. One by one, each child approached and merged with her. Sara was standing on the right, Sela on the left and again San Dy was in the middle. Sela and Sara were ready; San Dy decided not to stand in the way this time. Sela began to move toward San Dy on the one side and Sara moved toward San Dy on the other. There was a shimmering ecstasy that filled me, and, in a magical moment, the three of us became one.

On Wednesday, June 15, 1994, final integration occurred in the second floor office of Dr. Ben Keyes. On some level we three replayed the eternal... integration of mind, body, and spirit... one in three and three in one. It was a miraculous day. After arriving home, we drew us. I drew me. San Dy had become whole. I am not sure if I cried or if I laughed... maybe I did both. My heart made a sound that only the heavens could hear.

More to Do

Though I had experienced the most spectacular integration, my work was not finished. There was much that needed to be done to allow my oneness to connect with my life here in the present world. In all of my life, including the years in therapy, I knew I had never committed to being alive. Though I was now integrated and whole inside, I did not feel safe nor did I trust being on this Earth. There were still many lies programmed into my thoughts that had to be "unearthed," released, and replaced with truth. For six months, I continued therapy to heal Single Personality Disorder. On January 5, 1995, I experienced a particularly traumatic abreaction in Ben's office of an event in 1952 when I was almost eight, that had caused my child self to decide to end life. The reliving of that experience brought me face to face with that decision.

School was out for the summer in our town. My sister and I had gone to the schoolyard to play on the slide and merry-go-round. Daddy came to get us; he was angry, and his breath smelled of liquor. He ordered my sister to go home and began to spin me faster and faster on the merry-go-round. I became nauseous and begged him to stop. He finally did, but when he took me off, he took me to a hidden place and raped me in a particularly vicious way. There was no end... it would never end. There was no way to get away from the brutality that would go on forever, and since I could not end it, I needed to end myself. But I didn't know how to do that.

A short time later, my sister came home looking and acting strangely, telling my mother that she felt dizzy after she and a neighbor child held their heads over the tail pipe of a car that was idling as they sniffed in the funny smelling smoke. My mother was in shock and told her never to do that again! Mother told her that she could get so dizzy she would go to sleep and never wake up.

The old family car had no working heating system, often had bad tires and faulty brakes, and had a gas leak that came up from a hole in the inside of the car. We drove with the windows open on cold winter trips so the fumes would not asphyxiate us. After that horrible schoolyard experience, I decided to go to sleep and never wake up again using the information I learned from my sister's tail pipe experience. I slipped my head under the brown army blanket that we used to keep warm on those cold days and breathed in the fumes from the hole. My head got dizzy and I drifted into a deep sleep.

I woke up, both surprised and disappointed that I was lying on the side of the road with a brown army blanket under me. My siblings stood in silence beside the highway next to a tall grassy field. Mamma lied. I didn't go to sleep and not wake up again. A car pulled up and asked if we needed any help. Daddy told the driver that we just had a little car sickness. Daddy lied. Many years later, Daddy said that just before I came to consciousness, I turned over and vomited a long stool. I couldn't walk for several days, and had a headache that lasted longer.

Mamma stayed with me that night. We slept on a cot outside on the porch of a cabin so I could get fresh air. I remember her arms were around me as she whispered that she didn't know what she would have done if she had lost me. I didn't believe her tears. Over the years as I reflected back on that memory, I never understood why her arms and tears did not comfort me. She was a stranger. I had chosen to die, but fate kept me alive. Living wasn't my choice.

I had to reconsider that decision made so many years before. After that difficult appointment with Ben, I drove to my own office late in the night. I allowed myself to feel the excruciating pain of my child-self sitting in the back seat of our family car, no longer able to hold on to life. The choking pain filled me and I began bludgeoning a pillow with a baseball bat, something I encouraged many of my own clients to do in releasing anger. I beat the pillow and screamed at my father for all the cruelties with which he invaded every level of my life. I gave him back the lies he gave me and told him he would no longer have power over me. His violations had taught me to fear life, to hold it tentatively and let it go in the face of pain. He had taught me to trust no one and to expect that life was suffering. He inflicted many more lies on me.

Finally, in the exhaustion and exhilaration of that expression, I decided to choose life. I decided to allow the power of life to flow through me connecting me to Earth and to God. I made a commitment to life and now am feeling it committing back to me. After years of teaching empowerment to others, as a clinical hypnotherapist, working with adult survivors, and as an intern working toward a Ph.D. in psychology, I decided to open to empowerment- my own empowerment. In 1995, I knew that I had more work to do. Though my work was not finished, I had taken back my power and made a decision to choose life.

It is interesting to notice parallels. Shortly before that fateful trip to Washington D. C. where I met the man whose letters were lost, my husband had gotten angry with me for something I had said or done. I can't remember the cause of his anger. Perhaps I had challenged his authority. I went upstairs to take a shower. He came in, pulled me out of the shower, dripping wet, and lifted me over his head in a wrestling move. He carried me through the bedroom with me above him. I began to cry. I begged him to put me down as he approached the stairs.

A few years earlier, my husband, while playing roughly, lifted me up and began to carry me up the stairs to our bedroom when he dropped me down the stairs. The fall caused serious neck damage that took months to heal. This time, in spite of my tearful pleas to put me down, he continued down the stairs anyway. He walked across the hall and into the kitchen where he began spinning me above his head in a helicopter wrestling move. I pleaded with him to stop. I was getting dizzy and frightened. He dropped me on the floor and told me that now I would know who was boss. I was terrified.

I remember looking up at him with tear-filled eyes seeing a face that I didn't know; he almost looked possessed by some angry demon. Something inside me snapped. I remember feeling disconnected from the naked wet body that lifted itself off the floor, returned to the bathroom, and dried off. I made lunch for my husband and brought a tray to him in the family room where he was watching a football game. I sat at his feet and put my head in his lap. I asked him for forgiveness, though I didn't know for what. He didn't respond. Much later in therapy, I was able to connect the spinning in the schoolyard with the spinning in the kitchen. The part of me that was in charge could not handle being married to a man who had become like my father. She withdrew. This is when Jenny took charge to find a man who was capable of loving me. As I continued to work in therapy, other parallels between the childhood experiences and my adult-life became more visible.

I completed therapy with Ben in 1997, earned my Master's degree in 1999 and my Ph.D. in psychology in 2001. I became certified as a mental health counselor in Florida in 2002, and began traveling throughout the United States, and other parts of the world teaching what I have learned from my experience. I have since re-written the book *Melting the Chains*; the original attempt was too scattered. However, I have left some of it as it was written in 1992 as it reflects the scattered but more detailed story that is pictured here in this book. The pictures can tell the story, perhaps in a way that words cannot tell it. I have written many articles some of which have been published in professional journals and have completed the editing process for four other manuscripts, for which I am currently seeking publication. In 2003, a CD entitled *Healing*, which I recorded with Daniel Kobialka the world renowned violin virtuoso of the San Francisco Philharmonic Orchestra, was produced. Its intention is the same as everything I have written, spoken, or recorded, in the last fifteen years of my life, and that is to assist others on their healing paths.

It is my hope that those of you who are therapists working with survivors will be able to learn from the drawings, and perhaps find a way to assist your clients who struggle with dissociation. I am very sure you can learn from the awareness Ben reveals as he reflects on the various meanings he was able to find in the drawings. Each client has his or her own stories, and it is important to remember that clients will come together in their own ways because each one fell apart in his or her particular way. The maps that are presented here are mine, and other people's maps may look nothing like these. There is not a right way to draw a map. Whatever the client uses to express what is on the inside is right. The expression is what is important.

I also hope that those of you who are survivors in early, middle, or late stages of integration therapy, or in post-integration therapy might recognize symbols or energies within the drawings that set you free to understand and heal your own trauma. Perhaps, in some way this pictorial representation of my integration will help you to embrace the healing from your own wounds and you will feel encouraged to reach out, as well as within, to create your own *E Pluribus Unum.*

FROM FRAGMENTATION TO INTEGRATION

The Therapists' Perspective
Dr. Benjamin B. Keyes, Ph.D.

The mind map is a portrait of the inner topography of the self and as such can be an invaluable tool for the clinician in working with dissociative clients. Non-integrated trauma is generally unavailable to consciousness but can be accessed through drawing that produces an individualized road map for the therapeutic journey to healing. Mind mapping is a non-invasive, client-centered procedure that has the potential to ensure complete processing and integration of all the traumas related to the dissociation of the personality. This is an invaluable tool for any clinician working with clients who experienced childhood trauma resulting in repressed or dissociated memory and Dissociative Identity Disorder.

The mind map, as an effective technique in the consolidation of multiple or dissociated personalities, is presented herein from both the clinician's and the client's viewpoints in an in-depth, single-case study. A series of drawings produced by the client reflect the major steps in the integration process. The first map reveals over 250 fragments and alters. Each successive map reflects the consolidation process, culminating in final integration and a single personality. The photographs provide an overview of each full map as well as close-ups of significant portions that delineate the therapeutic process.

After completing integration therapy with Sandy, I encouraged her to collect her drawings and prepare a story of her integration. Slides were professionally prepared. Later, I was invited to present a paper on the mind map process on September 17, 1995, for the 4th Annual Conference of the Australian Association of Trauma and Dissociation Inc., in Melbourne. I titled this presentation *From Fragmentation to Integration*. It was well received.

In later discussions Sandy and I considered the possibility of bringing the two vantage points together, presenting the mind map system as a therapist's tool in guiding the process and a client's tool for bringing the unconscious into consciousness to facilitate healing. The result was the integration of the two papers in tandem with photographs of the drawings that were completed over a sixteen-month period from March 1993 to June 1994.

The Case

This work represents the single case study of San Dy S. San Dy had been referred to me through a fellow therapist who specialized in working with brief hypnotherapy but who did not want to make a long-term commitment to a client who had been previously diagnosed with Multiple Personality Disorder (now Dissociative Identity Disorder). San Dy had recently been trained in clinical hypnosis and had been looking for a therapist to continue and complete therapy she had started several years earlier in the Northwest.

From the beginning, this case proved to be quite complex and oft-times confusing in both its presentation and processing through therapy. It was out of that confusion that I began to ask San Dy to "map" the landscape of her internal system. Mapping is a technique that asks the client to draw or somehow represent either in symbol or word, aspects of the self that may show up as alters or fragmented parts of the self. This technique was used throughout the course of treatment providing guideposts, not so much for the client, but for this writer as a way of focusing and directing the therapeutic process. Often incidents of abuse, which were referenced to the specific parts of self, were confusing in the therapeutic session. However, these incidents became clear when referenced to the mind maps. Using the maps as guides proved not only useful in directing the course of immediate therapeutic treatment, but also in progressing toward final healing and wholeness.

My first exposure to San Dy's history came in the form of a 261-page manuscript, which she had written as an autobiography of her life. The manuscript proved to be insightful but it was inordinately disjointed in its writing and presented a fragmented history over time, mostly of her adult life. This writing was exceedingly difficult to follow. Her stream-of-consciousness style often had her flash back to periods of time in childhood and then attempt to correlate the flashbacks with current circumstances in her adult life. Much of the book was occupied in discussing issues related to her twenty-three year marriage and the effects of long-term early childhood sexual abuse on her life. Much of the focus was on the abuse uncovered in earlier therapeutic work she had done from the years 1986-1990. San Dy's fragmentation of writing style gave me insight into the fragmentation I would find within the internal landscape of her multiple system. It would occasionally provide me insight and glimpses that allowed resolution in areas of conflict that arose in the therapeutic process. Despite my having read her manuscript, however, it became extremely important for me to somehow try to piece her history together.

San Dy married at age 21, just after college graduation. She met her husband John in high school and dated him through her senior year and college. She committed to marrying him at 16, but even so had doubts when their wedding day approached. San Dy reported that she began having a recurrent dream that told her not to get married, but she felt that because John had seen her naked, she was obligated to be married. She had already made a commitment and needed to follow through on it. San Dy knew that something was missing in what she felt for him at that time and she wondered about the lack of closeness in their relationship.

John was drafted into the army one year later and went to Vietnam. He wrote to San Dy daily except during the TET offensive. During that time San Dy believed that he was dead due to a solid two weeks of non-writing. She relates a memorable experience of receiving 12 letters in one day at the end of that period and having simultaneous feelings of relief and also feelings of discouragement. Her husband was away for 2 years. While he was away, she lived with her mother until her husband came home; during this period she taught at a Christian school as finances were extremely strained. After her husband's return, she continued to teach for another ten years, stopping only because she couldn't keep her heart focused on teaching.

When her husband came home from the service he went to work and they continued their relationship. She continued to teach. Approximately one year after she left teaching, she started a commercial company and with her husband built it into a multi-million dollar venture. Once the company was up and on its feet, her husband took over the entire business and her position was relegated to that of a second-class citizen or employee. The year she left her husband and he took over the business, gross income dropped significantly to about half of what it had been the year before. It was just before she left the business that San Dy experienced the first "switch" of personality states. "Jenny" began coming out in 1985 and holding conversations with San Dy's husband.

Throughout the course of their 23-year marriage John had been verbally abusive and extremely critical of San Dy's weight and looks. He wanted out of the business and wanted to do something different. What that was wasn't ever really clear. When San Dy's husband took over the business she started to be involved in more public relations-oriented types of activities including volunteer work for a foundation. It was at a political dinner for that foundation that she became emotionally involved with another man connected to the group. She was both very afraid of wanting to be with another person and intrigued with the possibility of actually having her needs for love and acceptance met. After meeting at this political dinner and spending time together, San Dy experienced her first loss of time. There were periods of time when she would see this gentleman at a distance and the next thing she remembered she would be standing next to him holding a conversation. They continued correspondence for quite some time and would write to each other continuously.

San Dy kept his letters in an envelope in a file drawer in her office and one day it was gone. Shocked, scared that her husband had either found it or would find it, she sought out a therapist who was experienced in hypnosis to see if she could somehow remember or jog her memory through therapy and find the envelope. The therapist, who apparently was very skilled, clearly saw that San Dy was dealing with other issues and other problems and reflected that back to her in the therapeutic session. She never did find the envelope containing the letters but the encounter with the therapist encouraged and convinced her to begin treatment. Although the emotional relationship with the man was never sexual, it was nonetheless emotionally intense. Jenny, the one alter that she was aware of, very much wanted the relationship and when it was decided not to write to this man any further, this alter set out to attempt to establish another relationship to take its place.

The new relationship took the form of a gentleman from Atlanta who worked as a principal for a school and was certainly far enough away from the Northwest that the relationship could be kept distant and somewhat safe. During this period of time, San Dy would often get letters from both gentlemen and would continue correspondence with them. Often she would write or begin to write letters that she would leave open on her desk, clearly in a position where her husband could find them. She would be extremely shocked and embarrassed upon returning to her desk and finding these letters opened. She seemed unaware at times of these and other actions that were creating great havoc and confusion in her life. One day she came upon an envelope of letters that she had no knowledge of and found correspondence that she never remembered receiving or sending. As the loss of time increased she would also find herself in places and locations of which she was previously unaware. When traveling by car she was often confused as to directions resulting in five traffic citations within a two-week period of time. It was the combination of all of these events that caused her to continue therapy.

San Dy was with her first therapist for three years; however, a majority of the focus involved ego strengthening and trying to figure out how to disconnect from a marriage without dying in the process of doing so. Although the diagnosis of multiple personality disorder was given to her during this time, it was not directly worked with. Her first therapist moved to another state and San Dy stopped therapy for a while. More memories started coming back; flashes of parts of a life that she had forgotten long ago started to emerge.

San Dy found another therapist who specialized in post-traumatic stress disorder and multiple personality disorder and began a process of uncovering and discovery that continued to lead her on her path of recovery. San Dy's own words tell the story best:

> I began a journey into a hidden world that held memories related to the body messages that had been speaking to me all my life. Rape, pornography films, snuff films, drugs, electric shock, extreme abuse, several near death experiences were the horrors that were locked away in the back rooms and dark basements of my mind. Careful, caring work... helped me to unearth the causes of physical, mental and spiritual illness. I had to open the inner spaces, walk the corridors and enter the rooms that were the sanctuaries for frightened, separated parts of myself. Many had shown me the events that had sent them into their own darkness. I experienced the body responses as memories returned, often witnessing stigmata or feeling the physical sensations matching the physical trauma of thirty or forty years before.

During those initial years of therapy San Dy often required as many as five to six hours of therapy a week while her life crumbled around her. Marriage, her job, her belief system, and her sense of self were starting to collapse and to change and shift. She felt as if all foundations and structures had been shattered and through the cracks of the broken pieces, the flashbacks of the memory of her childhood began to come back. With her marriage collapsing, her relationships in flux, and the continued memories she made the decision to get out of her marriage and to temporarily leave the country by taking a job in the People's Republic of China teaching English in one of their colleges.

San Dy would spend two years away from the United States, relationships, and the world that she knew in a partial attempt to run away from the pain that she had been experiencing and also to "find herself." It was during her time in China that she began to study Chinese medicine and healing. She developed a stronger spiritual foundation and reconnected with her need to heal internally and grow spiritually.

It was in the late fall of 1991 that she returned to the United States, taking a job with a junior college in the State of Florida. The issues, the flashbacks and the memories, still unresolved led her to seek out therapy in February 1993 with this writer. It was at that time that we discovered that contained and locked away in the recesses of her mind were over 250 alters and fragments, splintered parts of her personality. I discovered that most of the previous work she had done had been in the vein of uncovering, working with and abreacting memories. There had been no attempt to consolidate or to work toward resolution of any of the uncovered material. The result seemed to me like someone oozing from open wounds that had not been properly covered or dressed.

Approximately two months after I began working with San Dy, I asked her to go inside to see if there was a safe place where she might be able to meet with a child part with whom I had been speaking. She described the safe place as a large open field with tall grass, and I asked if there were others who would come and join in the field. As San Dy looked around, she saw children peeking out of the tall grass and others scattered in various places, hiding behind rocks or other children. I asked if she would be willing to draw what she was seeing and that became the first mind map of her internal landscape.

What followed was a series of therapeutic sessions that focused on consolidation and the beginning of the integrative process. The drawings that follow show the progression from that first mind map through the process to the final integration. The pictures tell their own story of pain and trauma, the events that she survived in childhood and the wonder and beauty of the integrated self. The technique used predominantly for integration is a Christian technique entitled *Inner Healing,* which links the inner creative process to a spiritual awareness of God, however God is understood. God is present in the historical event as experienced in abreaction and in the client's future growth. This particular approach was consistent with San Dy's spiritual belief system and allowed her to work with the cognitive distortions resulting from the rigid dysfunctional fundamentalist Christian background in her childhood.

Post Integration

At this writing, in early 2004, Sandy has been integrated for over ten years. She is active, productive and has finished her therapeutic healing process. As with all of us, issues still remain. At age forty-nine she decided to return to school, and after five years of intense study, she received a masters' degree and then completed her doctoral program in psychology in

2001. In 1998, she decided to change her name by removing the split in her first name, and including the name Sela in her last name.

Dr. Sandy Sela-Smith is now a psychology professor and has a private practice working with many people including dissociative women who have experienced some of the same horrors and trials that she experienced. She is a gifted and talented therapist who is reaching many with her clear understanding of the journey and process of healing. It has been my privilege and honor to have had been a part of her experience and her healing journey.

Our commentary regarding the pictures provides a narrative of her healing journey and related issues, as well as personal reflections on the therapy. I would like to make one disclaimer. I am not an art or expressive arts therapist and, therefore, there are many things I probably did not see and continue not to see in the drawings. Still, the pictures and mapping led to a greater understanding of the internal process of this client.

THE MIND MAPS

THE MANY:

The Initial Map

BK: Showing four quadrants or areas divided in half with a pathway. The quadrants as you will see in the next photographs represent specific areas of work and issues related to the client. The map itself provides an overview of individual and system needs and issues.

SS: I drew this first map over a several day period. At the time I was renting a room in a house that felt very uncomfortable for me. I remember being afraid that one of the people who lived there would come home and find me drawing. I was not prepared to tell anyone what I was doing so I listened attentively for the sounds that would warn me that someone was coming. While one of the parts remained on vigilant watch, others drew. Though I didn't track the time, I know that on some level I dropped into the drawing and each part was actually drawing herself.

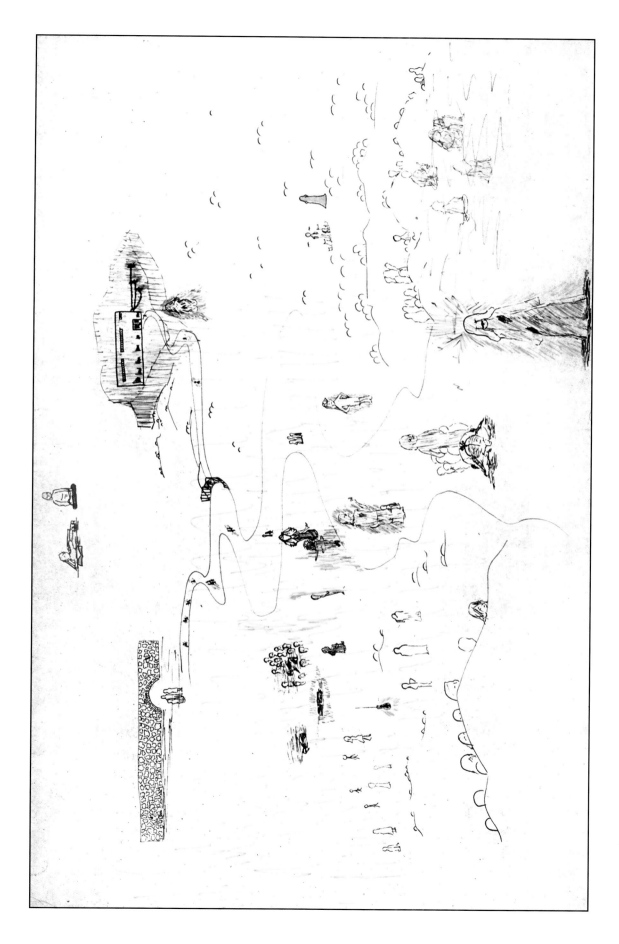

THE WALL

BK: Many alters are hidden here with an entrance that allows some to go out or in. These alters are wary of anything or anyone, and will take a "wait and see" approach to intervention or anything else. Very cautious. Far enough away that they cannot be gotten to right now.

SS: There were many children behind the wall. It was like a gigantic field hospital lined with cots. Children lay in various stages of being broken. Some near death, some whispering prayers pleading with God to let them come home. Angels sat beside the cots and held hands or touched brows as needed. These children didn't want to be here any more. Mary Eileen, Elizabeth and Ellen stood at the entrance to assist the passage into and out of the hospital. Some of the most wounded had never come out. Others had come out for a time but had been wounded again in my teen years and when I was married.

UPPER RIGHT QUADRANT

BK: Showing a well-protected and guarded compound. The pathway is fenced with a guardian at the entrance. Nothing in - Nothing out. Three alters chained to the building can be seen in the yard area. At this time, the client was unaware of what was inside, only that it housed the "monsters" and it was a fearful place - one to be avoided. Creatures, deformed, rancid oddities.

SS: I hated drawing the compound. It was surrounded by fire and a black impenetrable fence. I recall shaking when drawing this part of the picture. My stomach felt sick and I wanted to scream. The outer guard prayed for those on the inside but somehow knew her prayers were only to herself. She felt helpless to save those on the inside or to unchain the outer three but also could not allow anyone to enter. This was a place of the unspeakable.

THE FRONT LEFT QUADRANT

BK: Showing alters and fragments, mostly children. As was later discovered many of these represented single, varied incidents of abuse. Most not well defined, hiding.

SS: These were the children who experienced sexual abuse. The rape in the forest at four, the burial, the rape after the merry-go-round incident in the school yard that made me decide to go to sleep and never wake up. The light bulb I "went into" to not feel what was happening to the one on the bed... the little ones, the broken ones, the shamed ones, and the frightened ones. All are here.

THE FRONT RIGHT QUADRANT

BK: Again showing alters and fragments, most with poor definition, some hiding, some clustered, others isolated, some of the ones that are colored represent specific incidents of abuse. This quadrant had more of a feeling of isolation than the others.

SS: Extremely abused children are scattered between the front four and the prison compound. In the middle are Anna who protects the animals and her spiritual component in bright yellow. Many of these "hollow people" contained seconds or microseconds of memories of the most horrific inhuman abuse. The four in the front were the ones who together had made connection with the "host San Dy" and dealt with the outer world. Martha and Peggy had been co-partners for most of my adult life, Martha, on the far left at nine o'clock, responsible for John, and Peggy, at twelve o'clock, responsible for my professional life. Events in 1985 caused the shift in control to Jenny in the six o'clock position who wrote the letters that were "lost." Jennifer and Yvonne at three o'clock, were the shadow protectors. They had failed to protect me in childhood; they tried to protect me from what Jenny was doing by taking the letters but failed at that as well. They felt responsible for what had happened. The protectors turned on themselves and wanted to die.

The Initial Map

FOREGROUND RIGHT OF CENTER

BK: Alter who later became known as Martha - one who had to deal with husband, heart pain, stabbing wound, forgot forgiveness and God's presence to be able to seal the wounds.

SS: Martha was the alter who had moved to the host position following the disaster of 1985 and she shifted in and out of that position for a number of years. Only now she wore the scars of heartache caused by the shift to Jenny in 1985. At the time of this drawing, I was still in agony over the loss of my marriage, my husband, and my sense of direction that Peggy had provided with the pre-'85 Peggy-Martha alignment. Martha was alone. She had no husband, no lover, no direction. Without John she had no purpose. She was in pain and confusion and often felt the hopelessness of Jennifer and Yvonne. She felt truly alone.

THE MIDDLE SECTION

BK: The picture shows alters (again, mostly children). These later referred to specific issues and abuse. The angry alter in the middle questioned the "why" of any of the abuse. The protector alter of the children behind shows up in other areas, as well; that is a protector in front of other children.

SS: In the foreground, one child stands between a prone and wounded child and smaller children who are not capable of being there during the wounding. The protector looks to her left in search of someone to help the one who is hurt, but no one comes.

The first time and many times after rapes, the children longed for Mamma to come and make the "bad things" not happen but Mamma never came. After the first years of therapy I told my mother of the memories that had come back to me and the agony I was feeling without naming the rapist. She sat in angry silence and then denied that anything had ever happened to me.

She demanded that I tell her how such a thing could have happened and she not know about it. I looked at her partially in shock, partially trying to understand her and responded:

"Mamma, if I had a little girl who told me that she had been raped, I would have held her in my arms and asked her to tell me everything that happened and that I would protect her from ever having that happen again. . . and if I had an adult daughter tell me that when she was a child she was raped, I would hold her in my arms and tell her how sorry I was and ask her to tell me anything she wanted to."

Mamma continued to sit in silence. After waiting for something, anything, I began to cry and asked: "Don't you have anything to say Mamma?" Minutes passed. . . and I asked again, "Don't you have anything to say?"

Without responding to me for some time, my mother finally got up from her chair, walked behind me and put her arms around me like she did after the asphyxiation without speaking. My silent tears matched her silence and then she said. "Honey, If I had known, I couldn't have stopped it anyway, could I? So it really doesn't matter." We never spoke of it again.

The Initial Map

UPPER CENTER

BK: Spiritual alters - overseeing everything. Distant and removed from interaction with the rest of the system.

SS: I had always considered myself a Christian and believed I loved God but at the same time had a great fear of Him. I didn't like the "Christmas Jesus" because he was a baby and babies were helpless. I couldn't accept a helpless God; that was too frightening even to consider. I loved the "Easter Jesus" but ached inside because to have the Easter Jesus, I would have to acknowledge the Christmas one. Many sessions during the first three years of therapy dealt with my trying to understand who God is. Internal wars made finding the answer nearly impossible. God hated liars and I lied to my husband. I had committed adultery, there was no good in me and God would spew me out of his mouth. Even without the return of memories, the lives that my parents lead made me have little respect for them. I broke another commandment that required that I honor them. The God of my mother gave me no comfort and had no answers for the confusion in my life.

SHIFTS IN THE MANY:

The Second Map

BK: Again showing the quadrants, but this time more well-defined, interactive, and in closer proximity. Many of the fragments or as San Dy called them "hollow people" have integrated with the others and much of the internal landscaping is now known both to this writer and to the client. Specific alters are known with their functions and issues. These include but are not limited to:

Peggy: Organizer, child, six years old but seems to shift age as needed. First thought she was a teenager. Keeps cool and handles the situation. If things look as if they are falling apart, she takes over. She can make the good professional front.

Jenny: First thought she was thirteen, now seems ageless and shifts to all ages, Romantic, idealist, sees the good in everything.

Jennifer: Very depressed and related somehow to Yvonne. Both don't want to be alive, but there is not a sense that they would plan to carry out suicide either. Another child is the one capable of carrying it out.

Mary Eileen: Six-year-old whose job it is to care for the little ones.

Bonnie: Heard from once, father buried her after the rape. She was the one buried. Punished for telling mother about the rape. She says: "She belongs under the ground."

Major splitting here.
Martha, Emily, Ellen, Angel Lady called Sela (Internal Self Helper), Jennifer, shadow.

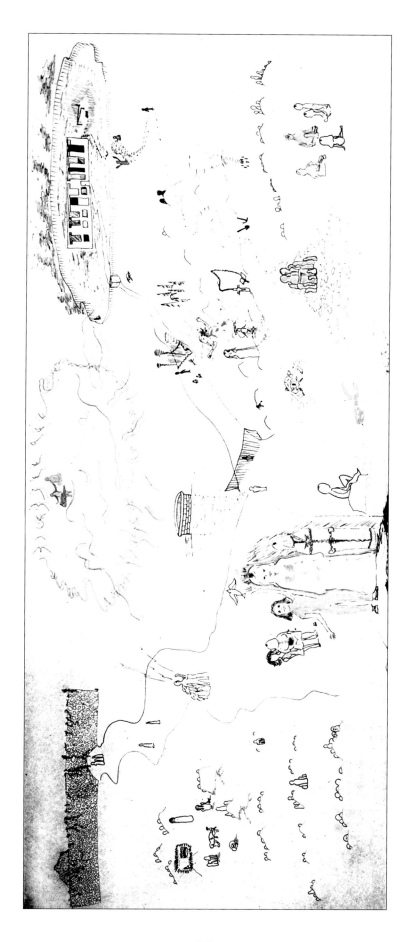

THE CENTER

BK: Depicts a number of things that turned out to be very crucial in the client's recovery process. The well in the middle led us to the discovery of levels within the system. The mapping shows the first level of alters, issues, events, conflicts. The second level deals with core issues of sadness, pain and horror and the third level relates to a pervasive melancholy throughout all aspects of the client's being.

The gateway to the compound is seen here more clearly and is now closer to other alters in proximity, letting this writer know that the issue contained within will soon be a part of the therapy process. In the foreground are Martha and Jennifer, as well as an undefined part sitting away on a stone. This alter was key to later work as you will discover.

SS: When I drew the well, I had no idea of its significance. It was in the center of the center and became symbolic for many levels of understanding of myself. Not only did it reveal the three levels of my system, it also was the representation of the pathway to the splitting. When an event at the external level (the well opening) was too difficult to handle, I dropped into the center of my center by falling into a deep shaft. This could be equivalent to dropping into the deep hypnotic state of the inner self. When I fell into the black bottomless place, alters were created who moved upward to take over connection with the outside. It was from this fall that I learned to get to the outside (out of body experiences, traveling to different places, different dimensions) by going deep into the inside. On the other side of the black hole was the outside. This symbolic fall was expressed in my body with horrible headaches in the top center of my head every time alter shifts took place or memories came back.

The Second Map

THE COMPOUND

BK: Greater definition of the compound. Notice that there are windows (hope). As we discovered, there were thirty-six creatures all deformed and disfigured. These creatures (many were children) related to abuse by multiple perpetrators, filmed by San Dy's father for child pornography. Most were extremely abused survivors, mutilated, hurt, and deformed. There are now two entrances (or exits) and ability to get in and out; also the guard is not as large (defending) and two others have taken over working cooperatively at the entrance.

SS: As I drew the prison compound, I found myself going into an altered state and entering from the right side door, not pictured. The bolted and chained double doors on the right in the first drawing had become a single door in the center of the building in this drawing. As I entered the dark corridor, I was aware that there were two floors with nine rooms on each side of the corridor, thirty-six rooms in all. I could hear the sounds of children. I had been here before in one of the last sessions with my first therapist. Some let me approach them, but most did not. The flames that had been within the walls had moved to the outside and the earth was barren and brown where the fire had been.

The Second Map

RIGHT CENTER

BK: This piece is directly related to extreme abuse with images of destructive conflict, with cognitive distortions related to God, Church and self.

SS: This was particularly excruciating to draw. One child representing many incidents of oral, vaginal and anal rape, the mirror image of the right leg pierced by the staple from the burial box, arms held down to inject drugs that made everything fuzzy and slow. A whirlwind pulls her in and she falls into the sorrow of another part of self that does not know what happened on the other side of the whirlwind. Tears flow into the blood streams of the Christ whose side was pierced and of a child who saw other children abused. The alter that watched the horror of this incident identified with the one who was being abused and took on the feeling of an empty hole on the right side of her face. Abreactions of this memory resulted in right eye blindness and a mirrored phantom pain feeling wherein the right side of my face felt raw as if a portion of it were missing but I couldn't touch it to relieve the pain. This is a feeling I experienced when I was under stress as long back as I can remember.

THE CHILD WHO STOPPED MOVING

BK: Incident of torturous abuse, with abusers standing around her in a circle. Notice the whirlwind of confusion.

SS: The child in the center of the circle lay very still. She learned to stop her heart from beating and her lungs from breathing. If she did not move, the energies could not connect to her life energy. It was only if she moved that they could enter, so she did not move. She didn't know where she learned to stop moving. She just knew.

The Second Map

ALONE

BK: Child alter who had been sodomized by father - tears, sorrow.

SS: She didn't know there was anyone else but her, alone in her pain, lying in her tears.

LEFT CENTER

BK: Mostly child alters who relate to individual incidents of abuse. Notice the positions, areas of abuse, and the "hollow ones" who continue to hide.

SS: These were the ones who carried the physical body-memories of the years of abuse. For over five years I had weekly and sometimes twice weekly body therapy sessions, which were for the most part based on a practice of deep energy work called Rolfing, which helped to release the pain and attached memories. Sometimes a session with my psychotherapist would lead to profound release of pain in the body therapy session and sometimes a body therapy session would access a memory that I had to deal with in psychotherapy. I carried the effects of the abuse in my body for my whole life until the healing released it.

The Second Map

LEFT FRONT

BK: Although these hollow ones are many, and seem to be more than the first mapping, the picture shows considerable consolidations and resolution. . . with many more to go.

SS: The rocks formed and the little heads hid behind them. I didn't know who they were or why I felt so empty when I drew them.

THE ANGRY ONE

BK: Again (shown from the first picture) an angry alter (not named) protecting many child alters and wrestling with the question why any of this had to happen.

SS: It was always difficult for me to access anger. Of all the visible alters in both drawings only one was angry in each. In the first drawing she seemed to be angry with the field of unidentified hollow people. In this map she was expressing her anger at the spiritual connection; somehow she blamed herself for not using what she presumed to be a higher and more powerful strength to prevent the abuse.

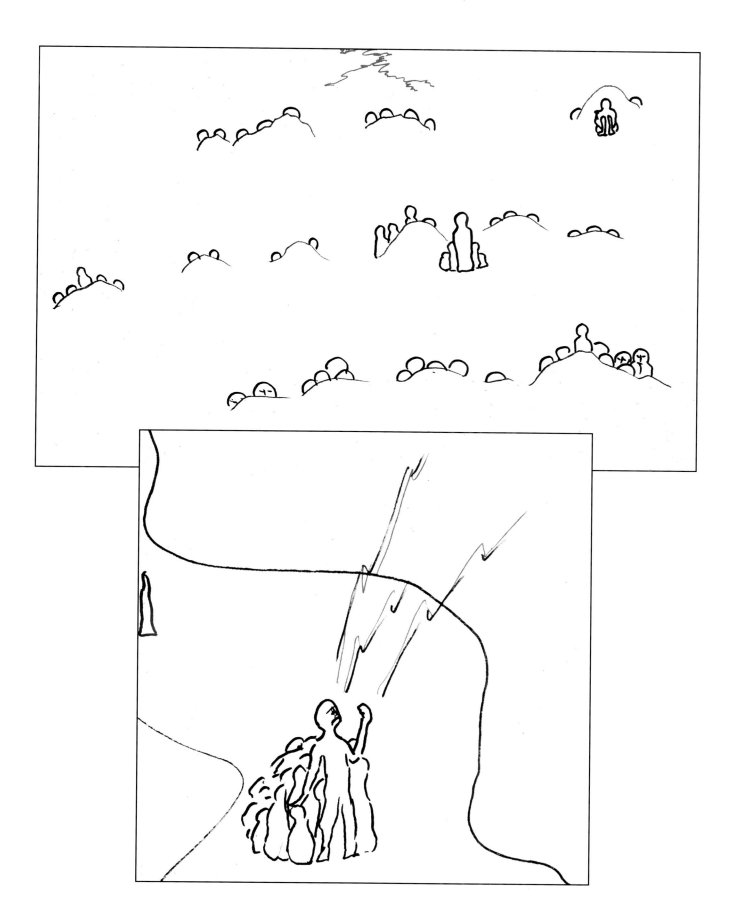

EMBRACING

BK: More clustering of alters, increase in trust and hope. Alters still not well defined here but as you will see these especially become more clear and prominent.

SS: Many of the children identified with animals. Animals could be loved and trusted. Humans hurt. There was safety in being connected with the animals.

THE FOUR PLACES

BK: These are the alters who represent voices talking in her head. Many alters previously referred to are present here. Communication has been established and cooperation within this part of the system is clearly taking place.

SS: Peggy, Martha, Jenny, Jennifer and Yvonne had not moved in place but their body positions had shifted. They seemed to be communicating and were not concerned with the hollow people behind them or anything else going on inside me.

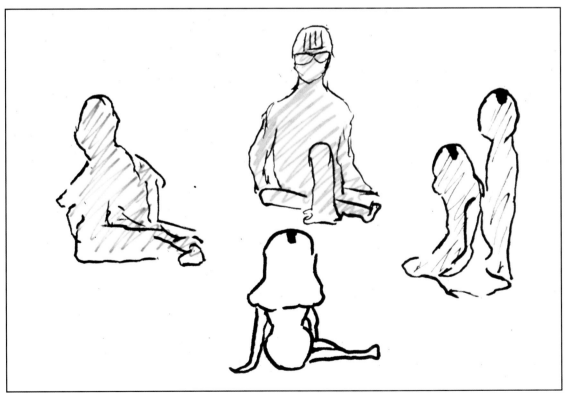

The Second Map

FRONT AND CENTER

BK: The child with the dove is Jenny, San Dy's lifelong companion. This is the undamaged, unhurt child who doesn't see existence through the veil of abuse. Hope, trust, love abide with this child. Notice two others behind, one with an ache and emptiness in the pit of her stomach.

SS: There were two energies closely attached to me: The Chained One and Jenny, the gentle hearted one. I loved Jenny dearly. When I first met her I believed that if I was to heal everyone and all but one would have to die; I hoped it would be Jenny that would be able to live. She saw and felt the world the way I wished I could, but my eyes had seen too much and my heart had broken too often. Behind Jenny stands fat San Dy covering up wild San Dy and protecting a child dressed up for a dance sequence in a pornography film.

THE WALL

BK: This time much closer to the rest of the system. Life has sprung up. Possibility and hope exist, alters still distant and removed but definitely watching carefully and learning as the therapy process continues. Notice also that life is starting to grow and spring forth inside.

SS: I was surprised to find ivy growing on the wall and a mountain in the background. I had no idea what was happening on the other side. I recall feeling somewhat happy when I drew this. I especially liked the single flower on the right corner.

TOP CENTER

BK: Spiritual part of self is much larger than before and starting to reach out to the rest of the system. Parts are closer in proximity to each other. Spirituality is becoming a larger issue in treatment. Distortions of God and self are coming up and conflicts with church doctrines and belief are part of the resolution process here. Client often confuses God the Father with God the Father who abused me.

SS: I had always believed myself to be a spiritual person but at the same time I felt like part of me was so disconnected from God.

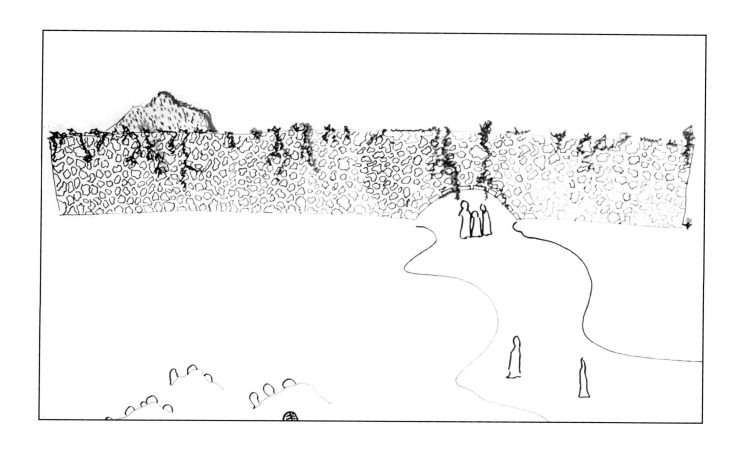

The Second Map

A FALL INTO THE WELL:

The Third Map

BK: Three months later San Dy was given the assignment to map once again. This time she was unable to draw and only able to write. Notice as you go through the writings that are pictured that the penmanship and writing styles often change. Color becomes an identification of issues. . . red, angry. . . yellow, spiritual. Also the voices, although not identifying specific alters by name, clearly point up the issues to be resolved.

SS: No matter how I tried, I couldn't make the pictures come. I was feeling particularly vulnerable. It felt as if there were conversations flying all over the inside of the whirlwind that was dragging me down deeper and deeper. Some were talking to me; others were talking to the ones who had just spoken. I heard the voices and as I dropped past them; I became the voices.

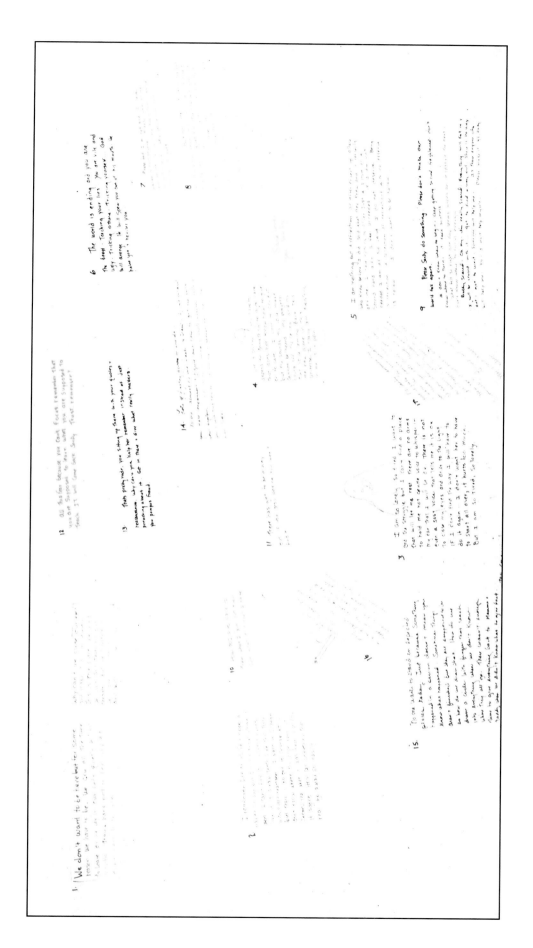

1. We don't want it to be here but too some

12. All this fear because you can't focus remember that you are Supposed to leave what you are Supposed to teach IT will come back Study first remember?

13. Faith pretty maid, you sitting up there with your quotes / resistance why can't you help her remember instead of just preaching about it God in place, Give what really matters you people found

6. The world is ending and you are to keep Teaching your life and ugly Tricking others Tricking yourself God will avenge it will eat you or as is worth it keep going, I see it, I see you

7. Prove me I'm here

8.

14.

11.

4.

10.

3. I am So lonely, So tired I want to Feel so strong but I can't find a place that will let me rest there are no arms to hold me not gentle voice to whisper in my ear a Soft Voice that tells me it's ok To catch my ears and cries to the light If I close like this way I will have to do it again I don't want here to have to Start all over, it hurts too much But I am So Tired, So lonely

5. I am nothing but a reflection of what you want me to be

9. Please Someody do Something Please don't make our world fall apart

15. To one wants to stand to expose

The following pages contain the statements made by parts of self who spoke as San Dy dropped into the well, followed by comments made by Ben, or both Ben & Sandy.

---

1. *"We don't want to be here, but for some reason we have to be. We cry all the time to leave or we lie in our beds quietly without moving, trying hard not to feel why we don't want to be here. Why can't we close our eyes and make it all go away? This is the place we wait. . . we wait and tears fill our throats but we mustn't cry. We stare out at nothingness and wish to go with our eyes."*

BK: You can hear this; the soulful cry of the parts of self, the unresolved conflict, and the cognitive distortions. The mapping, whether in picture or in written form, gives the therapist a direction for treatment and specific clues as to what the work is. Alters, with joined or separate voices, are calling for help, and, finally, connection is established for aid and healing; finally, needs begin to be met.

Notice the shape of the wall - it points to the issues they (the others) contain.

---

2. *"I remember one of us felt hope a day or so ago, but I don't know where it went. I can't find it. My chest hurts like it is a raw toothache that throbs with every heartbeat. I want to scream but there is no one to scream at; I don't know where the hope went. It seemed real when it was here, but now it is gone. How can something that is real go away so easily?"*

1. We don't want to be here but for some reason we have to be. We cry all the time to leave or we lay in our beds quietly without moving. Trying hard not to feel why we don't want to be here.

Why can't we close our eyes and make it all go away. This is the place we wait... We wait and tears fill our throats - but we mustn't cry. We stare out into nothingness and wish to go with our eyes.

2. I remember one of us felt hope a day or so ago but I don't know where it went. I can't find it. My chest hurts like it is a raw tooth ache that throbs with every heartbeat. I want to scream but there is no one to scream at. I don't know where the hope went. it Seemed real when it was here, but now it is gone. How can something that is real go away so easily.

3. *"I am so lonely, so tired. I want to end the struggle but can't find a place that will let me rest. There are no arms to hold me, no gentle voice to whisper in my ear that I will be OK. There is not even a soft voice that tells me it is OK to close my eyes and drift to the light. If I don't find the way I will have to do it again. I don't want to have to start all over, it hurts too much. But I am so tired, so lonely."*

BK: San Dy has done much study in comparative religions and the reference has to do with the issue of reincarnation and having to experience life over again. The call, the drive is to resolve her issues this lifetime, this time around. Drawing of alter is well defined with facial features.

---

4. *"Life is painful. . . you have to depend on something to give care that does not know how to give or to care. I want to cry out but the sounds my voice makes cannot be heard. My prayers bounce off the ceiling and my own voice, coming back, tells me how alone in this universe I really am. Everything in me is pain."*

3 I am so lonely, so tired. I want to end the struggle but I can't find a place that will let me rest. There are no arms to hold me not gentle voice to whisper in my ear that I will be ok. There is not even a soft voice that tells me it is ok to close my eyes and drift to the light. If I don't find the way I will have to do it again ... I don't want her to have to start all over; it hurts too much. But I am so tired, so lonely.

17.

4 Life is painful ... you have to depend on something to give care that does not know how to give or to care. I want to cry out but the sounds my voice makes cannot be heard. my prayers bounce off the ceiling - and my own voice coming back tells me how alone in this universe I really am. Everything in me is in pain.

5. *"I am nothing but a reflection or after effect of others who knew before I did, and said what they knew, and it reflects off me. I have nothing to offer, just a picture of a second hand gift. I feel unneeded. If I am not needed; I am of no value. I do not deserve. Being a reflection. . . a collection of reflections with no essence. . . is hollow. I do not want to be hollow."*

BK: This particular writing was done by the Host, San Dy, as she became aware that she also was an alter, one part of a system; her purpose was to see and reflect what the others knew and processed. She questioned her self and her function and wondered if she was but a shell and if she had substance. For several sessions we worked to resolve the conflict arising from her awareness of being an alter along with others.

SS: When I wrote this I thought I was referring to the belief that I had spent my whole life mirroring other people's wants and beliefs. I thought I was nothing in myself. Somehow, if everyone decided at once that I was not there, I would no longer exist. This was a painful awareness for many years. The more I learned how much I didn't know who San Dy was, the more I believed I was nothing but a reflection. When I read Ben's interpretation of the words, I understood that we were both correct. My sense of self was hollow both from the outside and the inside.

---

6. *"The world is ending and you are the beast. Teaching your lies, you are vile and ugly, tricking others - tricking yourself. . . God will avenge. He will spew you out of his mouth. He hates you and reviles you."*

BK: A condemning part of self.

SS: My religious upbringing taught that there was a beast that would engage in a violent battle with God in the end times. I had moved away from fundamentalism and embraced a much broader spiritual understanding that made room for the possibility of reincarnation, a vision of a loving God, an acceptance of the goodness of man's heart. I believed in love instead of fear. My spirituality was alive and God connected for the first time in my life, but a part of me was terrified by the new beliefs.

5   I am nothing but a reflection. an after effect of others who knew before I did, said what They Knew and it reflects off me. I have nothing to offer Just a picture of a Second hand gift. I feel unneeded. IF I am not needed I am of No value. I do not deserve. Being a reflection - a collection of reflections with no essence is hollow -   I don't want to go hollow.

6   The world is ending and you are the beast. Teaching your lies. You are vile and ugly. Tricking others - Tricking yourself... God will avenge. He will spew you out of his mouth. He hates you + reviles you.

7   Please God. I'm no
wanted to hurt anyone. P
and see me. I cry. My
to hurt anyone. Why u
       who loves.

7. "Please God, I am not bad. I never wanted to hurt anyone. Please look at me and see me. I cry. My heart never wanted to hurt anyone. Why would you hate someone who loves?"

BK: Part of the incongruence here has to do with the client's conflict with her mother. Mother was a domineering, controlling person who would often use subtle manipulation to get her own way. She taught rigid legalistic Christianity while flagrantly violating its tenants with coldness, and lack of love or empathy. Also during extreme abuse, San Dy often saw others being hurt and believes some were killed. She was forced to participate.

---

8. "My head hurts. The God of the end of things that will come in and kill all the people and turn the moon into blood and fill the river with blood and send Jesus to kill all those who don't know the name of Jesus. . . that God scares me. Maybe there is another God on the other side of that one that really does love everyone. I want more than anything to believe in the God of Love. It would hurt me to think of someone having to go to Hell. Wouldn't it hurt Him more? He is much more love than I am. Oh God, please, please help me. How could you spew me out of your mouth if you love me? Dear God. Do you hate me as much as mamma and daddy hate me?"

BK: Again, the distortion of reality can be seen. Messages from Mother and Father were confused with the teaching of love in Christianity. The Christian teaching was that God will spew you out of his mouth – the teaching was targeted at unbelievers. This scripture was often used for control purposes by mother, both internally and externally.

7 Please God. I'm not God. I never wanted to hurt anyone. Please look at me and see me. I cry. My heart never wanted to hurt anyone. Why would you hate someone who loves.

8 my head hurts. The God of the end of things that would come in, kill all the people, Turn the moon into blood, fill the river with blood, send Jesus to kill all those who don't know the name Jesus... that God scares me. Maybe there is another God on the other side of that one that really does love everyone. I want more than anything to believe in the God of Love. If it would hurt me to think of someone having to go to Hell, wouldn't it hurt him more. He is Much More Love than I am. Oh God, Please Please help me. How could you spew me out of your mouth if you love me. Dear God Do you hate me as much as mamma, daddy hate me?

9. *"Please San Dy do something. Don't make our world fall apart.*

I don't know where to begin; things keep getting shifted. Frightened. . . don't know where to turn. It feels pointless.

What felt so right one day feels wrong or impossible the next. Don't know where to focus energy.

Really scared. Everything will fall in and I will be crushed with it. . . got to find a way out, got to wait, someone will help me. . . Is there anyone who will help me. . . No I must help myself. . . please make it go away. "

BK: Notice the different handwriting, and the changes in color. Four separate voices, turmoil, conflict.

SS: Coming from the right front corner, Jennifer and Yvonne, Peggy, Jenny and Martha cried out to host San Dy to do something. Nothing seemed to be working any more. It hadn't really worked since 1985 when the Peggy-Martha administration collapsed into the hands of Jenny. They all wanted me to help but I didn't know how.

---

10. *"How do I give back to them when I am not even sure what it is that I have?"*

BK: Questions of giving to others inside and increasing the communication system. Confusion about knowing what to do or how to do it. Not knowing within the self how to give back to the self.

SS: Ben again saw this statement related to the inside. I saw it related to the outside. How do I give back all the lies that I took in from my parents, from the other perpetrators, from religion, from society, when I am blind to what I believe? Again, both are true.

a reflection - a collection of reflections with no essence
is hollow - I don't want to go hollow.

9   Please Sandy do something. Please don't make our
world fall apart.
    I don't know where to begin - keep getting shifted - freightened - don't
know where to turn - it feels pointless.
    What felt so right one day seems wrong or impossible the next -
don't know where to focus energy.
    Really Scared - Oh my - I'm really scared. Everything will fall in r
I will be crused with it ... got to find a way out. There is no way
out - got to wait - Someone will help me - Is there anyone who
will help me. no. I must help myself - Please make it go away.

10 How do I give back to
them what I am not even
sure what it is that I have.

11. *"There has got to be a way out. If you stop looking, you won't find it."*

BK: The spiral in the background corresponded to the spiral with the whirlwind and its three system levels.

SS: So many times in the years of therapy I wanted to give up. It seemed like a hopeless search for wholeness. Sometimes the pain was so great I wanted everything to end. . . but something in me kept going.

---

12. *"All this fear because you can't focus. Remember that you are supposed to learn what you are supposed to teach. It will come back someday. Trust. Remember."*

BK: A spiritual alter is reminding San Dy that there is purpose in all of this and that fear is created because focus is lost. She is chastising as well as bringing a message of hope.

---

13. *"That is pretty rude, you sitting there with your quotes and reassurances. Why can't you help her remember instead of just preaching about it? Get in there and give what really matters you pompous fraud."*

BK: An angry alter who despises spiritual niceties in the face of horrible reality. Angry at what she sees as prayer without backbone.

11   there has got to be a way
out. IF you stop looking you won'r
find it .

12   all this fear because you can't Focus. remember that
you are supposed to learn what you are supposed to
Teach It will come Gack SonDy Trust. remember?

13.   Thats pretty rude, you sitting up there with your quotes +
reassurances. why can't you help her remember inskad of just
preaching about it. Get in There + Give what really matters.
you pompus Fraud.

14. *"Lots of fighting going on inside. No one, almost no one wants to draw. If we draw you make comparisons and figure out how to fit us into your system. Not going to spend a whole session letting you figure out how to box us up and finish us off. No way Doctor!"*

BK: This alter is clearly upset at not only the process of mapping, but the internal shifting going on. The alter is under the false belief that as integration took place, other alters died. Also a struggle against what was perceived as my agenda in working with the map. Client is becoming more aware of how I am working; as you will see next, there is a clear reminder that what I see is not all there is.

15. *"No one wants to stand in expected places today. Just because something happened in a session doesn't mean you know what happened. Sometimes things are not finished, but they are supposed to be, so how do we draw that? How do we draw a circle with fingers that reach into everything when we don't know where they all go? There wasn't enough time to give everything back to mamma and daddy when we didn't know what to give back. Too Confusing!"*

BK: The latter part of this refers to work done in several (many) sessions identifying and looking at the negative messages given to her in childhood by her parents. The focus toward the end of these sessions was on giving the negativity back to them (as it was theirs) and beginning to realize that these issues were theirs not hers. Clear admonitions to this writer that some things were incomplete, overlooked, and possibly rushed. Many sessions spent retracing steps to complete the process. I was often confused by issues and situations presented and found that at times the more I tried to understand and make things logical, the more illogical they got. I allowed the process to unfold, often without direction. When I got out of the way, things seemed to clear up to a point of resolution, both between alters and concerning various issues.

14. Lots of fighting going on inside.
No one - almost no one wants to Draw. If we draw
you make comparisons + figure out how to fit us into
your system. Not going to spend a whole session letting
you figure out how to box us up + finish us off. No
way Doctor.

4   Life is painful... you have to
      ___ Something to give care

15.   No one wants to stand in expected
places today. Just because Something
happened in a session doesn't mean you
know what happened. Sometimes Things
aren't finished but they are supposed to be
so how do we draw that. How do we
draw a circle with fingers that reach
into everything when we don't know
where They all go. There wasn't enough
Time to give everything back to Mamma.
Daddy when we didn't know what to give back.

3   I
end t
that
To h
my e
even
To cl
IF I
do it
to st
But

too confusing!

16. *"How do I make my soul not lonely? I don't know how to play or laugh. Laughing drops me deeper into the hollow place. I want to go back to the stillness and go with my eyes into the nothingness."*

BK: The Host's call to stop the hurt, the pain; a call to rest.

SS: As long as I could remember I was aware that there were always tears under my laughter. If I allowed myself to laugh from the deepest place tears would flood the laughter. Safety seemed to require not laughing from my center.

---

17. *"No San Dy , remember how good it feels to give workshops and watch the changes. Even though you think you hate doing it, you like it. I know you think about it in the future. Planning months ahead, you feel trapped by the lines on the calendar. How can I get out of the traps I set for myself? Let me just go away. . . Oh stuck again. Maybe if I sleep."*

BK: The organized professional part wants to remind San Dy of the good feelings she has had about her therapeutic work with others and her professional plans for the future. At this moment the host was feeling trapped and stuck, and decided to end the map by going to sleep.

SS: Drawing the word map made me very tired. I had been through a whirlwind of emotions, feeling all of them in my body as I dropped into the well. As so many times in the past, though this time I was hearing and feeling the voices rather than experiencing trauma or triggers that caused switching, the fall made me exhausted. The only way to end the exhaustion was to sleep. So I did.

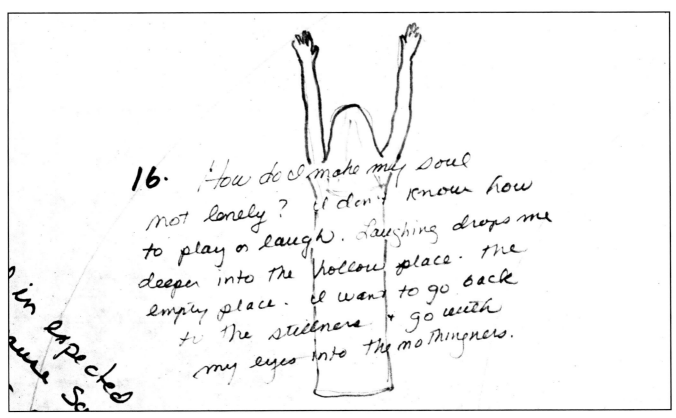

16. How do I make my soul not lonely? I don't know how to play or laugh. Laughing drops me deeper into the hollow place. The empty place. I want to go back to the stillness + go with my eyes into the nothingness.

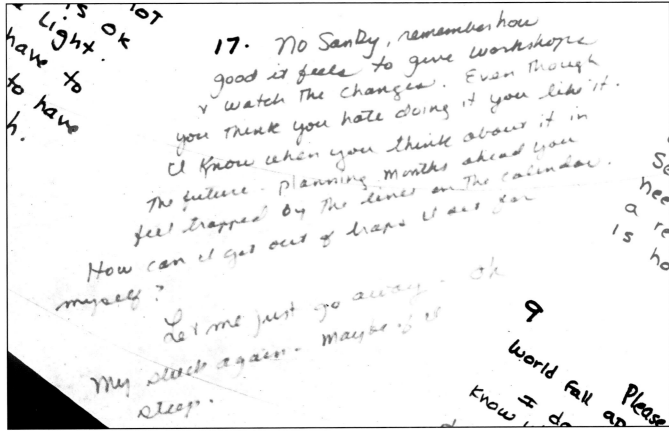

17. No Sanky, remember how good it feels to give workshops + watch the changes. Even though you think you hate doing it you like it. I know when you think about it in the future. planning months ahead you feel trapped by the lines on the calendar. How can I get out of traps I set for myself?

Let me just go away. ok My stock again. maybe I'll sleep.

CONSOLIDATIONS:

THE FOURTH MAP

Approximately six months later.

BK: Notice the consolidation of the quadrants and clustering of alters. There is increased communication internally within the system and increased cooperative organization. Gone are the areas of the compound and the wall; much of the individual abuse issues are gone and resolved. Considerable integration and fusion of alters and fragments has occurred at this point. Roadways, pathways are no longer necessary. Issues are starting to be clustered within specific alters and groups of alters. The three levels, anger, pain, and fear are visible; melancholy is very predominant in the work. There is much confusion concerning issues related to father and those related to husband. Many of the patterns were similar. Confusion continues to be represented by the spiral with a clear internal call to be rescued (see the area of the wall).

BK: | Unresolved incidents of abuse. Witnesses, parts, etc.

BK: Horror and fear still present with anger hidden beneath a whirlwind

BK: Many of the previously named alters are here in full and clear definition; their proximity and relationship to one another can be clearly seen. Notice also the changes in colors, which are more vibrant and alive. Also some alters are clearly smiling.

SS: From left to right in the front are Martha, Jenny, Peggy and Yvonne. I was beginning to understand the roles the four had played in the Jungian quadrangle. Peggy was the "CEO", queenly director personality, Jenny was the Romantic personality, Yvonne was the shadow side of warrior-protector energy and Martha held the shadow side of my creative, magical energy. Her fear made her rigid and fearful of challenging tradition. I was teaching a course on empowerment about the time of this drawing without realizing that my four had matched the names I had given to the four Jungian-based positions in personality. . . Direction, Protection, Connection and Creation. Behind these four were the splits and shadows or shadows of the shadows.

BK: Mostly children, still afraid, withdrawn; fearful of the hurt, the unresolved trauma. Notice the whirlwind, the spiral that continues underneath and extends from the core of this group.

SS: These are the ones who feared the sounds of footsteps, and the turning of doorknobs. They dreaded the exhaustion that came from late night wake-ups and trips to awful places. I often heard their voices crying in the night.

BK: The Inner Self-Helper, Sela; in the middle, involved with the system, no barriers, Jenny - light side. Jennifer - dark or hurting side seen in proximity to each other and close to integration here.

The Fourth Map

SELF PORTRAIT

BK: Separate drawing of androgynous self, lonely, alone, sad.

SS: After a body therapy session in which I had felt the right side of me go into mournful sadness for not being strong enough to protect my left side from having a needle put in my arm, I felt especially out of balance. My right arm felt weak but seemed to want to protect my left arm that was exceedingly heavy. The heavy, sluggish left arm wanted to cover my genital area that was in pain. My head felt out of focus, out of balance, almost as if two people had been melded together and did not know how to fit. I was sick for a time after this drawing.

———————————————————————

PAIN

BK: Again, separate drawings of parts of self. Self-portraits of parts missing areas of hurt, sorrow, isolation and melancholy. We had reached the third level at this point and began working with the pervasive melancholy.

SS: Memories coming back impacted my physical body. Pain even went into my bones, creating the feeling of tiny fissures and hairline cracks everywhere. I drew what I felt like from the inside. There were so many times it felt like it would never be finished, never be better. . . hopeless.

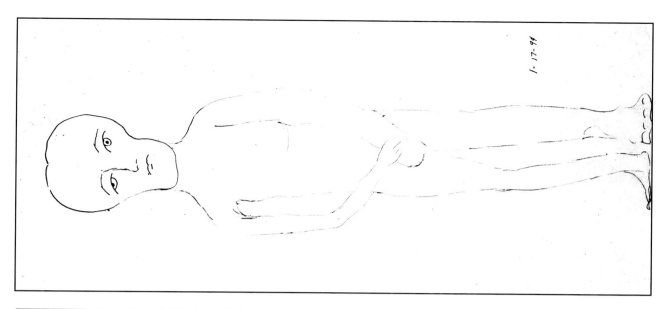

The Fourth Map

COLLAPSE OF THE LEVELS:

The Fifth and Sixth Maps

FIFTH MAP

The fifth map shows only part of the entire system as you will see in the next photograph, which shows the sixth map. Notice here the collapse of the levels. (They no longer exist in the system). A considerable amount of resolution of abuse incidents shown here, much work with cognitive distortions completed at this point, especially those related to parents. Sela (the Inner self-helper) no longer on high but is present in the middle.

The Fifth Map

SIXTH MAP

Shows further consolidation of alters, but also showing the dark side not seen in the previous drawing. Sela again is seen in the foreground with Gabriel, the confronter behind her. Only nine alters internally at this point. Two children, two adults in the foreground, two children, one young adult, and a dark alter to the side, and San Dy.

BK: The broken one with the Dark one, child who feels like "shit" and believes she is made of feces. As we worked we found that Yvonne, a teen, was convinced that death was the only answer to this horror called life. Every time she looked out she saw darkness. The other two children related specific events of abuse by Father; anger, sadness, fearful. Sexual fondling, remembrance of seeing a man burned to death.

Working with the energy of the dark one-produced stigmata; the client was choked in childhood. Red hand markings appeared on her neck and face in the session. Increase of memories tied to extremely violent abuse of others.

THE DARK ONE

BK: Notice there is no voice, lack of movement, a sense of confinement, locking away of sexual energy, which starts to be an issue in therapy with thoughts of again being in a relationship. Client is terrified.

SS: The one standing behind Yvonne contained the darkness that the teenager could not allow herself to look at or into. The dark one contained all the horror and had to be kept separate. The belief was that looking into it and really seeing it would cause death. When we finally worked with this child, I found her in a vile place where, after a perpetration, she had been smeared with feces.

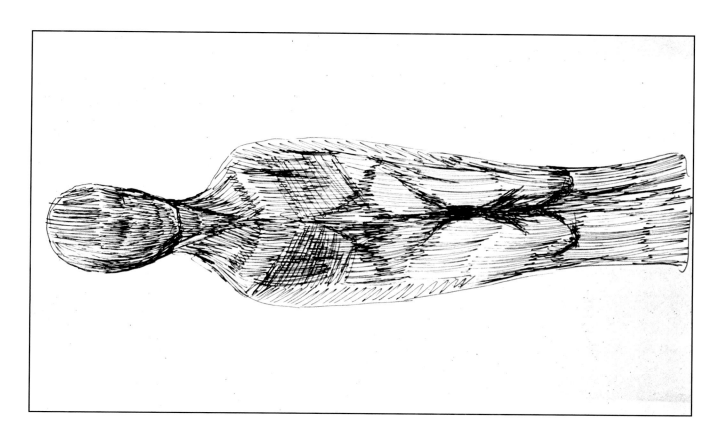

THE WRITING OF TEEN YVONNE:

A dialogue between San Dy (the host) and Yvonne.

Y   *If I open my eyes, I will see the black beside me and hear the tears under me, and the screams behind me. I must be as still as I can. Maybe they won't notice that I am here.*

S   *What would happen if you stood up and looked directly into the black?*

Y   *I will die.*

S   *How do you know?*

Y   *Because I did, oh, I did. I can never do that again.*

S   *Where did you go when you died?*

Y   *I went into the blackness, I fell and fell into the blackness. The blackness is icy cold and fire hot. It swirls without stopping. It burns you up until there is nothing left and it is lost. Oh it is terribly lost. It is lost and doesn't know how to come back. I close off the icy cold fire. I won't feel it, I can't. I won't look into the blackness. No one can make me. . . or I'll be still.*

The child is very fearful of everything being consumed by the darkness including her very soul. The last comment suggests that if she does nothing or remains still it might all go away.

If I open my eyes, I will see The black beside me and hear The Tears under me, and The screams behind me - I must be as still as I can. maybe They won't notice That I am here.

What would happen if you stood up & looked directly into The Black?

I would die

How do you know?

Because I did - Oh. I did. I can never do That again. I

Where did you go when you died

I went into the blackness. I fell and fell into The blackness

The blackness is icy cold and fire hot. It swirls without stopping. It burns you up - until There is nothing left. But something is left - And it is lost. Oh it is Terribly lost. ... It is lost and doesn't know how to come back.

I close off The icy cold fire - I won't feel it - I can't. I won't look into the blackness.

No one can make me - you can't make me - I will scream inside my head so you can't make me - I will be still

FROM NINE TO FOUR

BK: Sela, Gabrielle, Emily, happy free child and her opposite who is sad and hurt.

The Sixth Map

THE SEVENTH MAP

Four alters in three separate areas. Notice at this point, except for the whirlwind in the very right corner, the entire map has life and aliveness throughout. Sela and Emily in the front. The sad child by the lake; one of the children who sat by the rock is now up but dealing with the darkness. She is Sara.

BK: Incident of abuse when the child was buried in a box and tied with a rope. Again the presence of stigmata. . . severe rope burns appeared around her ankle. Confusion, the resolution of this event allowed the whirlwind to cease its presence in the system and the child to integrate. Connecting to the dark place related to the box. (She was placed there for punishment and was anally raped when released.)

BK: Sad child.   Removed, away, believes safety is in the isolation, fearful.

BK: Sela, the inner self-helper, spiritually giving to the child who is open to receiving.

AND THEN THERE WERE THREE:

The Eighth Map

Sara, Sela and San Dy.

BK: Sela, shown with the representation of the integration and other parts of herself. San Dy and Sara. Notice that Sara is now turned facing the group. The eyes are still wary and not sure if she should trust or not. The group is joined by arms. The movement toward unity continues and at this point the alters are bonded together.

SS: I was aware that there seemed to be three parts of me. It occurred to me that Sela and Sara might see things differently than I did so I asked them to draw us. Sela drew us all three connected. Arms stretched out with Sela and her spiritual helpers and angels providing loving support. Sara was with us but looked to her left with fear.

SARA'S DRAWING

BK: Sara (child from the lake in the previous series of pictures) is now much closer. She is turned away but much closer.

SS: Sara drew the three of us with herself turning away in what seemed like shame and sadness without a mouth to speak. She saw Sela and San Dy as connected, she separate.

_____

BK: Sela, from the eyes of Sara.

_____

BK: San Dy and Sara.

5-17-94
Sela drawin
Sela
SanDy
Sara

BK: Sela overlooking what San Dy has to deal with. The mind of San Dy, if you will. San Dy's struggle to deal with all the plates spinning in her life has often been overwhelming. Money, school, relationships, possibility of home, travel, and public speaking. Not to mention what is not listed, dealing with parental issues, cognitive distortions, self-esteem, and body image, among other problems.

SS: I asked Sara to draw what made her feel so separate. She drew two pictures. One was of Sela and San Dy. She saw Sela as radiant, spiritual and eternal and San Dy as someone with a future filled with lots of things going on, difficult but with potential.

The Eighth Map

BK: | Close up of San Dy's mind.

BK | Sela. Notice the radiance of the free spirited child within. Expansive in-out reach and scope and beckoning to San Dy. Many sessions with Sela attempting to spiritually teach, cajole, awaken San Dy to look beyond the immediate circumstances.

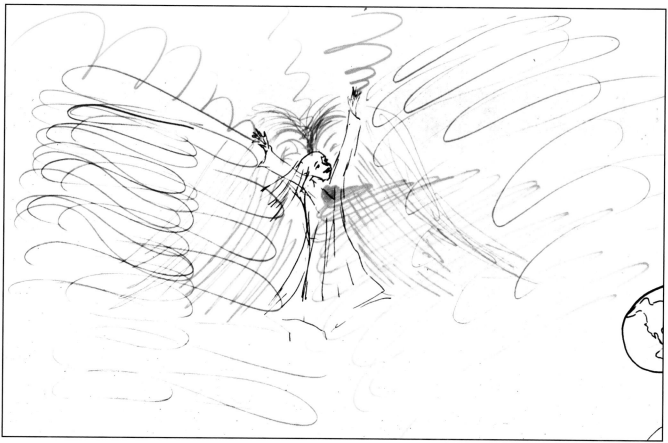

The Eighth Map

BK: Sara believed she could not be a part of San Dy and Sela because of what she carried. She carried the pictures of past scenes of abuse, the box she was buried in - placed during extreme abuse - which was similar to a coffin. Other abuse with a knife, and videotaping of child pornography. All flowing and known now to San Dy. San Dy is attempting to put things in some perspective.

SS: Sara drew why it was that she could not connect with Sela and San Dy. She carried the horror of what was done to her; she carried the physical, which she believed was evil. Sara believed she was condemned because she was physical. . . she was finite, sinful and would turn to dust. She believed she could not free her body of the internal scars, the energy scars that were her inheritance. Burial places, hiding places for horrors, events that could not be changed.

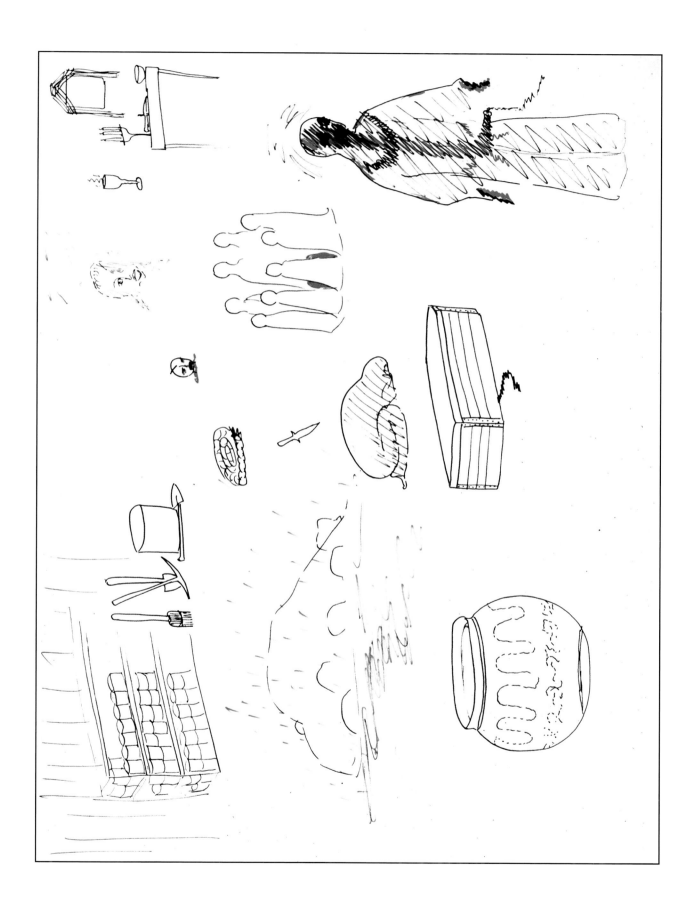

BK: A closer look at the images previously described. Note the lower right corner showing the figure of father abuser. Distortion of self-image and self-blame for her abuse.

BK: Places where some of the damaging objects were hidden, remembrances of a tortured past that was now being assimilated into a future and into moving on.

The Eighth Map

SHAME

BK: This picture is simply titled "shame". It represents various poses of a naked child who had to perform (sexually and in pornography) to be loved and accepted.

SS: This was a painful picture to draw. It was even more painful to have it exposed. I did not bring it in to show Ben after I had drawn it. After integration, when I decided to do the first photo shoot of all of the maps, I did not photograph it myself. I had intended to pull it from the collection of maps after my own photographs did not turn out and I decided to have the work done professionally. I hadn't gone through the maps for some time and had forgotten to remove this one. When I noticed it among the others, I felt myself gasp. Even after integration, I still had work to do on shame related to my body.

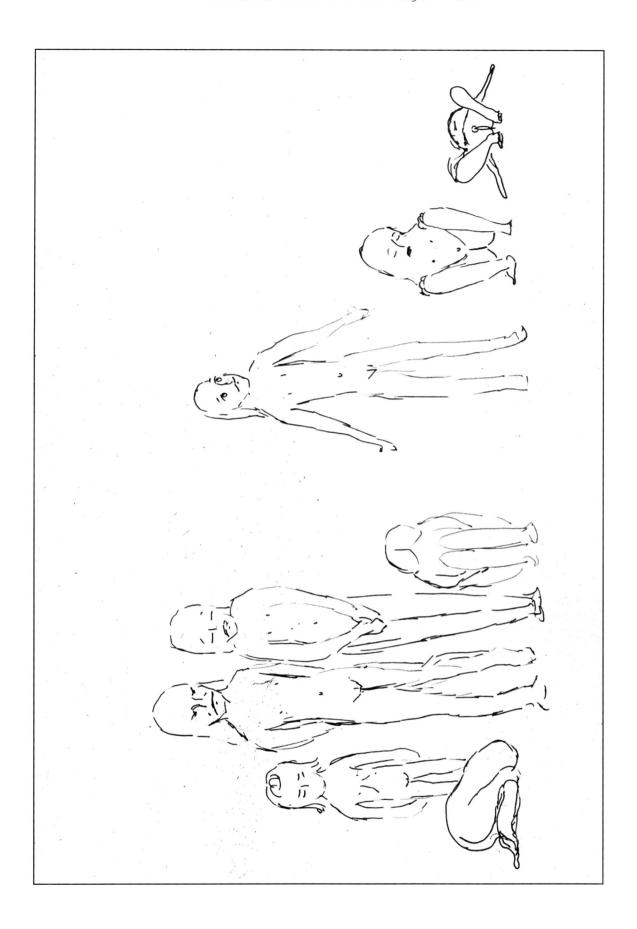

AND THEN THERE WERE THREE

SELA, SAN DY, SARA

BK: The barriers have dropped at this point; all issues are being worked to resolution. Little demarcation between the alters as movement, communication and cooperation are shared and working.

SS: This was my favorite drawing.

I could feel the flow of love among the three remaining parts of myself. All of the work seemed to have brought us to a place of mutual respect. Sela was my spiritual awareness, Sara my physical self and San Dy my mental expression. . . and yet somehow we all contained each other.

REMEMBERING
HOW IT USED TO BE:

Reflections of the Old Self

SS: Nearly a year-and-a-half had passed since I had drawn that first map with over 250 parts and splinters of myself. Just after having completed that first drawing, I was aware of how distressed my body was feeling. I decided to draw a picture of what my body felt like so that my body therapist could help me work with the extreme pain that made living a difficult task. I felt as if invisible hands were pressing down on me, forcing my shoulders to collapse against my chest, making breathing an exhausting experience and making my bones ache. My mouth felt muzzled and my arms felt shackled. Blocks and pressures kept me from feeling any sense of flow in my body and in my life. I didn't feel connected to my legs. So much had changed in the months between the first drawing and the last!

BK: The old self-concept; drawn at the time of the first mapping, dark, unloved, shackled sexually, tortured, wanting to die. The self of old has finally metamorphisized to:

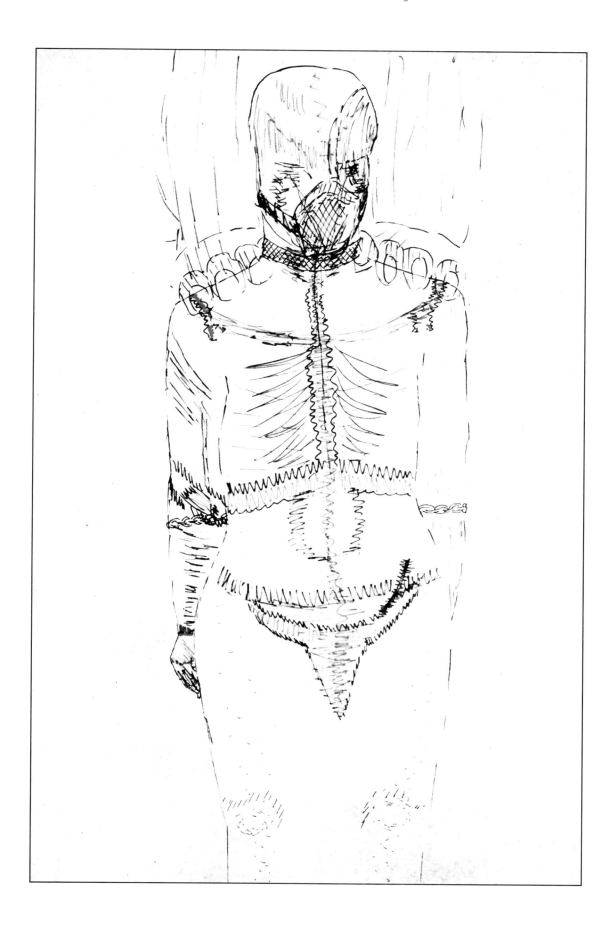

OUT OF MANY. . . ONE:

The Final Map

June 15, 1994

BK: A unified, integrated, and alive self is formed. The final picture does not represent the end, but a wonderful, growth-filled, living beginning.

SS: When I left Ben's office I was in a state of ecstasy. I couldn't believe how beautiful everything in the world looked. Colors were richer and deeper. Birds sang more beautifully, and I felt more alive than I had felt as far back as I could remember. I was in such a state of joy I wanted to record it in some memorable way, so I found a piece of paper, and I drew a self-portrait. At the time I had a small peach colored parakeet that often sat on my shoulder, a dog named Sara who was the light of my life, and a feisty calico cat named Rachael. All of them belonged in my drawing of light and life.

The Final Map

After drawing what was to be the last picture in my process,
I took out a second sheet of paper and I wrote a poem.
It seems appropriate to include it here.

ONE DAY

When I began my work, I was told that One day I would wake up in
the morning and be so glad the morning had come.

One day I would be able to laugh
without tears under my laughter.

One day I would discover the joy of child-like play
without fear of allowing myself to be vulnerable.

One day I would be able to sit in a room
without needing to keep the entrances and exits in view.

One day I would be able to walk in the forest, hear the sound of
footsteps, watch the turning of a doorknob, see
silhouettes in the evening and not have panic fill my
heart with unknown terror.

One day I would be able to choose whom I want to be with
instead of being with them only because they chose me.

One day I would be able to curl up in a lover's arms and feel safe
instead of hearing thoughts I don't understand, thoughts
that would make me want to cry.

One day I would be able to remember every thing that happened
in a whole day without even trying.

One day I wouldn't have to keep track of distances and times to be
sure no time was lost, except when I forgot to remember.

One day I would be able to ask questions in a conversation
because I was involved instead of carefully listening to
try to cover up that I didn't know who the people were
or what they had been talking about.

One day I would be able to live life spontaneously
If it hurt I could cry, if it was funny I could laugh,
If I was angry I could yell, If frightened
I could call out - and if I wanted to be loved I could be.

One day I wouldn't be at war with myself. . . Or with God
I would like who I am. I would know that I am
perfectly imperfect, that my essence is pure and good,
that it is ok to make mistakes, that I don't have to
make everybody like me, and that I don't have to
save everyone else in order for myself to be saved
I would know that I am lovable, worthwhile,
valuable, worthy and that I deserve love.

I woke up this morning and am so glad my one day has come.

AFTERWORD

1995

Sometimes we have no idea how far we have come until we allow ourselves a moment to turn around and notice our journey. This is my moment. In preparing this manuscript, I read Ben's account of my integration process. I wept. The tears were not really tears of sadness, though there was sadness in them. They were not tears of joy, though there was joy in them as well. They were tears of relief, tears of wonder, wonder in the remembering of years of pain that seemed like they belonged to another life, another lifetime. Over a year had passed since my integration and my life was filled with Ph.D. work, with plans for study in Brazil, with prospects of making room for a man in my life.

I was considering invitations for workshops around the U. S., balancing all of this with my growing practice in Florida. I had become so involved with living that I had almost forgotten how it used to be. I had forgotten about the horrible falling apart years while working with David, and the excruciating year of memory retrieval with Steven. . . the year that brought me close to ending it all on more than one occasion. I had never before fully understood how I had experienced multiplicity all of my life, and how the host called San Dy had maintained the outer shell so carefully, and then fell apart in 1985.

I had not thought about the alters for months, except perhaps for Sela who was both alter and spiritual connection, higher self. (When I work with clients or practice spiritual healing, I continue to shift into Sela awareness). I had forgotten about Peggy, Jenny, Mary Eileen, Yvonne, Jennifer, Anna, Bonnie, Emily, Ellen, Evelyn, Elizabeth, Martha, Sara and many more as separate from me. As I read Ben's first draft wherein he stated that I had married my husband in spite of the fact that I had not loved him, I realized that it was Jenny who did not want to marry him; Martha did, though it was Jenny who fell in love with John in high school when he gave her the electric blanket to keep her warm. Jenny wanted to be loved by someone who could look into her eyes and see her soul. After John went away to college, he did not know how to look into eyes anymore, and after he returned from Vietnam, he seemed not to be able to look into her heart anymore. She became painfully lonely. Martha had promised to marry him when she was sixteen; she would not break the promise.

As I reflected back to that time early in my marriage when my husband left me on Halloween night, for the first time I realized that it was Peggy who held everything together, helped him shop for furniture and waved good-bye as his pick-up truck rounded the corner, and it was Yvonne who collapsed when he disappeared into the night. Jenny fell in love with the Canadian man who could look into her eyes and who wrote letters offering entrance into the inner sanctum of his soul. Mary Eileen made the men Jenny connected with promise not to be sexual, and it was the four-year old, Bonnie who fell into the black hole when the "local man" did not keep his promise.

The host, who maintained the balance in the system from perhaps high school on, was not able to do so after the letters were lost. She had no conscious knowledge of Jenny, Jennifer, Martha or Peggy. She had no conscious knowledge of the deeper levels or the memories held by the younger ones. All San Dy knew was that her world was crumbling and she had no idea what made her do the things she was doing. She became aware that she was losing time. She was terrified.

With the crack in the system, deeper levels of alters became terrified as well. They had been able to contain their memories, maintain the inner checks and balances, and create a semblance of normalcy until the crack created all new threats that no one knew how to handle. Deeper-level, younger alters began to struggle for control as San Dy became incapacitated. When this happened, San Dy suffered periods of amnesia. Each shift in the power struggle occurred with piercing headaches and depression. San Dy had lost control. Some begged her to regain her position and make it like it used to be. That was no longer possible. Others demanded that she step aside and allow them to take over. They were not competent. Major system failures occurred internally, which negatively affected San Dy's entire outer world. Yvonne sat for days in the Papasan chair staring into nothingness and Jennifer tried to die when the pain of memory and collapse became too great.

Sela was the Angel Lady, San Dy's higher self who first visited San Dy when she was buried in the box at four and gave her strength to survive the years of torture that were ahead. The first major split occurred during the rape when San Dy tried to turn into a stone to stop the brutal act but was unable to. The burial which followed was the birth place of Bonnie, Martha, Emily, Ellen, Mary Eileen, Elizabeth and the many others who lived in the blue stone structure too wounded to live and too weakened to die. Extreme abuse caused major splitting that created those who lived in the fire-encircled compound. A particularly torturous event created multiple splintering which was then followed by splintering of the splintering that accounted for the formation of the hollow people.

Reading Ben's account and writing my own memories of integration allowed me to understand the falling apart more clearly than I had ever seen it before. My tears were expressions of compassion for myself for what I endured, perhaps for the first time truly claiming that the drawings I had done over a sixteen-month period were drawings of my self, and that what happened to the little girl, happened to me. I can now own my story. I can tell it; it, too, has become integrated. It has woven itself into the me that I have become, and the me I have become is far more than the story. When I first began the deep internal work in therapy, a "future" San Dy promised all of the parts that no one would die. I kept that promise. I am Peggy, Jenny, Jenny-Marie, Jennifer, Yvonne, Martha, Mary Eileen. . . I am Emily, Elizabeth, Ellen, Evelyn. I am Sela, San Dy, and Sara. I am all the named and the unnamed. I have come far on my journey. I am one. . . I Am. . . For this, I am grateful.

November 5, 1995
San Dy Smith

AFTERWORD

2004

It has been approximately ten years since Sandy integrated and seven years since the completion of the initial draft of this manuscript. Since that time I have seen hundreds of dissociative clients in inpatient, partial hospital and outpatient settings. Sandy's experience stands out to me as one of the most triumphant from the standpoint of, first, her artwork, and second, her incredible journey towards success. Following integration, Sandy went back to school and completed a doctorate in clinical psychology. She is in a full-time private practice and is teaching for a noted graduate school. Her story and her example show what can be done in the healing process and are a wonderful illustration of the fact that we are limited only by what we can conceive and by what we are willing to devote ourselves to accomplishing. Sandy's story is not unique, however, in that many men and women who have come through the healing process have gone on to lead full, successful and productive lives. It is to their memory that this work is dedicated.

In his Foreword, Dr. Colin Ross indicates that this work might generate some controversy regarding the techniques used in the therapy. He also states that the irrefutable evidence of healing is its own judge. I have always believed that any clinician doing good therapy need not worry too much about controversy, as good therapy can only serve the clients' interests. As counselors and clinicians we have been blessed with an enormous responsibility - to facilitate healing for our clients and to be a conduit for their growth and development. I have always been clear that the healing work is done by the client and not by the clinician, and that we clinicians are but vehicles for the clients to use in the healing process. If controversy is generated by this book, then so be it, but I have never gotten into the validity of the clients' memories, since this is their subjective experience. I have always been supportive of the clients' process and their understanding of their histories and experiences, which will often change throughout therapy, sometimes in context and sometimes in structure. My having the foundation of the client's context allows the process of therapy to be neither invasive nor iatrogenic. Understanding, insight, and integration of the material occur in the realm of the client's process.

My own professional career has taken a number of turns since the years when I worked with Sandy. I have had the opportunity to travel abroad to teach therapeutic techniques for working with dissociative disorders. In 2002, I traveled to Shanghai and Beijing, China with Dr. Colin Ross to teach clinicians there how to work with dissociative disorders and identify their etiology. This was the first such teaching ever to occur in China. We both found the Chinese to be excellent clinicians and researchers who are struggling to bring their nation into the twenty-first century, and to adopt modern treatment protocols and standards of care. The invitation to China came after six years of collaboration and preparation. With our Chinese colleagues we conducted a large epidemiological study of the prevalence of dissociative disorders in Shanghai. This research was a replication of earlier work by Dr. Ross. I have been told that we will be asked to travel to China again, likely in 2004 or 2005, to teach the psychiatric community, and I am very much looking forward to the experience.

I also have had the opportunity to teach at conferences in Australia and throughout the United States, and I have a profound interest in a Christian focus on inner healing, as I believe it parallels the work done with dissociative disorders. I have been extremely grateful for where this work has taken me both in my own personal journey and in my professional life. I trust that the journey will continue as I plan to continue doing workshops and meeting with clients. I hope one day to teach counseling skills within a University structure and to pass on my abilities to those who will come behind me to continue the work.

I am so very grateful to the many clients who have opened their hearts and minds and allowed me the honor of traveling with them in their healing. I have rejoiced and cried at their amazing strength and resilience in overcoming seemingly insurmountable obstacles in their healing and their lives. They have brought peace, joy and love to the world. This book is a work of love and I hope it provides inspiration to those who are questioning whether the journey can be successful or not. Sandy's journey continues, as she pursues her teaching and works with her own clients as I do with mine. I will always be pleased and honored to be in her presence.

Benjamin B. Keyes
March 21, 2004

AFTER THE AFTERWORD

2004

A year or so after my integration, sometime in early 1996, I was struggling with painful, embedded beliefs regarding the unacceptability of my body. The inner conflict was related to the memory of a particularly horrible wounding at my father's hand. I re-entered the traumatic situation, brought present awareness into the past belief, and asked my child-self's father if he was sorry for what he had done. There seemed to be no remorse whatsoever. That father of so long ago seemed to be cold and impenetrable. I suggested that I no longer wanted his energy in and around me and released my father to the angels to teach him what it meant to take responsibility for his treatment of me.

In this deep conscious state, I saw in my inner mind a gigantic 'sixteen-wheeler' truck pull up beside my father, and a huge, very determined-looking angel get out. This powerful angelic being opened the trailer door to expose a full load of boxes. Some of the boxes had my name on them. The boxes were filled with the records of the damage my father had caused, not just to me but to others as well; each was labeled with incidents and names; some names and labels were familiar to me, and others I didn't recognize. The angel picked up my father as if he were a small child and put him in the one remaining space in the back of the trailer. This powerful being then rolled down the trailer door, went back to the cab, and drove away. I felt relieved that my father was gone.

While still in the altered state of consciousness, I wanted to go to the place where the angel had taken him. I found myself on the other side of the universe approaching a huge warehouse; it was by far the biggest warehouse I had ever seen. The last of the boxes from that truck were being unloaded. I could tell that these were the boxes from this lifetime. They were being added to boxes from other lifetimes that were stacked from floor to ceiling as far as I could see. The angel assigned my father the task of clearing the warehouse. My father was to personally carry each box, one by one, to some other place, with no help from anyone. It looked like a task that would take an eternity. It felt important to move beyond that time into the future to see how things were going. It seemed that much time had passed, and I returned to see my father sitting on the floor, looking extremely weary, leaning against a stack of boxes in a warehouse about half full now. He painfully got up, picked up another box, placed it on his back, and walked out a door into total blackness. I had no idea where he was going.

I asked to be taken forward in time again to the time when he was finished with the task. When I returned, there was only one box left in the massive, echoing warehouse. My father picked up the last box, put it on his back, and walked out of the door. I decided to follow him. He stumbled along a path that was filled with broken rocks, up one hill, and down the other side, only to climb another, and another. In total exhaustion, he laid the last box on the ground, next to a shadowed, rough plank, and fell to his knees. I looked up, and in the silhouette of the dusk-filled sky, I saw the form of a man, head bowed and looking down on my father, arms outstretched, and nailed to a wooden cross. I was in awe. When I began this journey, I had no idea it would lead to the figure of Jesus. Tears streamed down my face; my whole being experienced the magnitude of what was happening.

After he lay down the last box, his eyes looked up into the face of Jesus and my father sobbed in remorse for what he had done. Jesus spoke in gentle tones, proclaiming my father's forgiveness and in that very moment, we were back in the totally empty warehouse. The ceiling dissolved in front of my eyes, the walls collapsed, and the floor turned into thick black earth from which the most beautiful flowers and rich green grass emerged. Trees grew up and were filled with birds and the sky was clear blue. Mountains appeared and a waterfall and river flowed nearby. It was the most breathtaking view I had ever seen. My father's arms rose into the air; his head fell backward, eyes looking skyward, as powerful, bright, beautiful laughter poured out of him. My heart was filled with joy. My father was finally free.

As 1996 was coming to a close, just before Christmas, I received a telephone call that my father was in an operating room fighting for his life. I closed my eyes and took a shamanic journey to meet him in an alternate reality where I saw him floating above the operating table as surgeons worked on his body. I told him that I had seen the future time when he laid down the last of his burdens. I wanted him to see the beauty of the moment when his heart opened to forgiveness. As he lay there above the table, his head tipped slightly back, I heard him laugh. It was a beautiful laugh of joy, of release, just as I had seen him do in the empty warehouse during that healing journey a few months before. It seemed very important for him to see this picture just at that moment.

I asked my father if he would be willing to survive the operation so I could talk to him in physical form and told him I would be taking the next available flight. I tried to see into the future beyond the operating room, but all I could see was blackness. I felt tears streaming down my cheeks. I tried harder to see, but could only see a gray form sitting in a wheel chair with tubes all over him and I knew my father would not survive the operation. I completed my spiritual conversation with him close to around 1:30 PM Eastern time. A short time later, I received another call from my sister. At 10:31 AM Pacific time, my father passed away. For those few minutes I saw him floating above the table in my vision, he must have just left his body. I made arrangements for a flight the next day. There was no funeral for him and my mother chose to spend Christmas alone.

For many years of my life, buying Mother's Day cards was very difficult. I wanted to be able to give her something loving, but my heart struggled with a need to tell its truth. In the years following my father's death, I focused much of my inner work on my experience with my mother. After much painful work around my life with Little Sandy's mamma, I was able to forgive her for being too afraid to challenge her husband. Forgiveness was possible when I discovered that I carried the same fear in my marriage and forgave myself for actions based on that fear. In May of 2003, I sent a Mother's Day card to her, recalling the event when I was not quite eight years old and had nearly died of asphyxiation. I thanked her for pulling me out of the car so very quickly in time to save my life, and I thanked her for lying beside me on the cot telling me how much she loved me. I had finally been able to feel the love that she did have for me, a love that my child self could not feel because of the pain, a love unfelt until I had forgiven her. My mother cried when she received the card. Two months later when I flew home to celebrate her birthday, I held her in my arms and told her how much I loved her. My love for her was real; it flowed out of a healed heart and I know she knew it.

While working through issues with my mother and father, I also worked on the heartache of my failed marriage. Unresolved pain related to my husband that still lived in my heart, my mind, and my body at the time of my integration became healed as reflected in much of what I wrote in the intervening years between 1994 and the beginning of the new millennium. So many of the deeply spiritual principles related to the meaning of life and the people and events we draw into our lives became clear to me as I worked with issues around John. As I learned with my parents, when I forgave myself, I could forgive others, including him. I believe that the two of us joined together in this lifetime to heal deeply buried wounds, and as a result I released so many embedded beliefs that wrote too many life-scripts for me. I feel so free, and I thank John for his contribution to that freedom. Without his playing of the role he took in my life, it might have taken many more lifetimes to learn what I learned in those 23 years with him and the years of healing afterward.

Through intense therapeutic work, the child who was born with a split name became whole in June of 1994, and 4 years later that split name changed, as well. In the fall of 1998, while working with Dr. Frank Lawliss, author and therapist, and Dr. Jeanne Achterberg, internationally known for her work in visualization and healing, I experienced another shamanic journey. I was taken to a circle of spirit beings who told me that it was time to take a new name. I was also told that the power of my first name San Dy, meaning helper of mankind in Greek, had been weakened by being split at my birth. I was supposed to remove the split in my first name, and then attach Sela to my last name. Sela, a Hebrew name, means rock or stronghold, like a fortress, a place of protection. My last name, Smith, is British and describes one who re-shapes or transforms things. I discovered that the name was identifying the transformation of myself from helplessness to empowerment, from weakness to strength, and from insecurity to security by creating connection to the power that comes from integration. In October of 1998, I applied to the court system and I officially changed my name from San Dy Smith to Sandy Sela-Smith.

I would never choose to experience such abuse again, nor would I wish it on anyone. However, I now realize that one of the many gifts that were left on the doorstep of the abuse, was awareness of deep levels within myself that I may not have known about had I not been forced to flee into them. What I know of myself in relationship to the Universe and what I know of the profound resources we all hold within us as human beings was gained in the process of surviving those horrible early years. This knowing that comes from experience has become the focus of my work now. Currently, I am researching deeper levels of awareness to facilitate not only psychological healing but physical healing as well.

As Sela told Sara many years ago, the physical is the visible expression of beliefs held by the emotional and mental self. Only when hidden beliefs are manifested in the physical, can there be any hope for them to come into conscious awareness, which then opens to the deepest levels of transformation. My life is full, though at times I feel emptiness; I am joyfully happy and on occasion I can feel deep sadness. I know I am loved but occasionally I don't remember. And I know the truth of who I am, in spite of the fact that from time to time I forget. I celebrate the fullness, the joy, the love and the truth and I am most grateful that in the process of healing, as I promised myself nearly 20 years ago, I have not lost a single part of the many parts of me that for so long believed themselves to be separate. . . but now know that they are all a part of me, and I am one.

Not until the final editing before going to print did I notice that my new name was derived from the languages of three significant cultures. The Greek culture is one that offered the world philosophy and wisdom, while honoring the right of the individual to self-rule through reason and democracy. This contribution opened the way to thoughtful self-reflection of mind and personal responsibility. The Hebrew culture offered the world a religion. Like all religions, it provides the structures of human conduct, but also contains the possibility of leading the devout to embodied spirituality that knows we are all one through love. And the English culture stimulated expansion of the physical, material world into a single culture through domination. However, once domination is finally released, unity that had been experienced through force has the potential to be experienced with choice. These three names in one, Sandy, as mind, Sela, as spirit, and Smith as body can represent one small part of the much greater transpersonal transformation of all humankind into One. Integrated oneness allows all parts to responsibly live together through self-examination with mutual respect, honor, and love, without the loss of a single part. To envision what can be is to open pathways for the vision to become a reality.

Dr. Sandy Sela-Smith
June 15, 2004

A NOTE TO THE READER

The authors invite you to write to them
by regular mail or by email to let them know
how this book has affected you.

Dr. Sela-Smith:

Sandy Sela-Smith
PO Box 4744
Clearwater, Florida   34601

selasmith@aol.com
ssmith@tampabay.rr.com

Dr. Keyes:

Benjamin Keyes, Ph.D
PO Box 106
Florida 33779

drben@tbi.net

Website:

www.infiniteconnections.us

Both Dr. Ben Keyes and Dr. Sandy Sela-Smith are available for evening presentations on the subject of healing from Dissociative Identity Disorder as represented in *E Pluribus Unum: Out of Many... One*, and they offer weekend workshops on Inner Healing.

If you are interested in more information on possible presentations, please contact them at the above addresses.